PART ONE

(VERNAL EQUINOX)

Volume One:
Out From Boneville

Jeff Smith

Cartoon Books
Columbus, Ohio

THIS BOOK IS
FOR
VIJAYA

Acknowledgements: The Harvestar Family Crest designed by Charles Vess.
Color by Elizabeth Lewis.

For information write to:
Cartoon Books
P.O. Box 16973
Columbus, OH 43216
or
ask@boneville.com

Hardcover ISBN: 1-9636609-9-3
Softcover ISBN: 1-9636609-4-2
Library of Congress Catalog Card Number: 95-68403

10 9 8 7

Printed in Canada

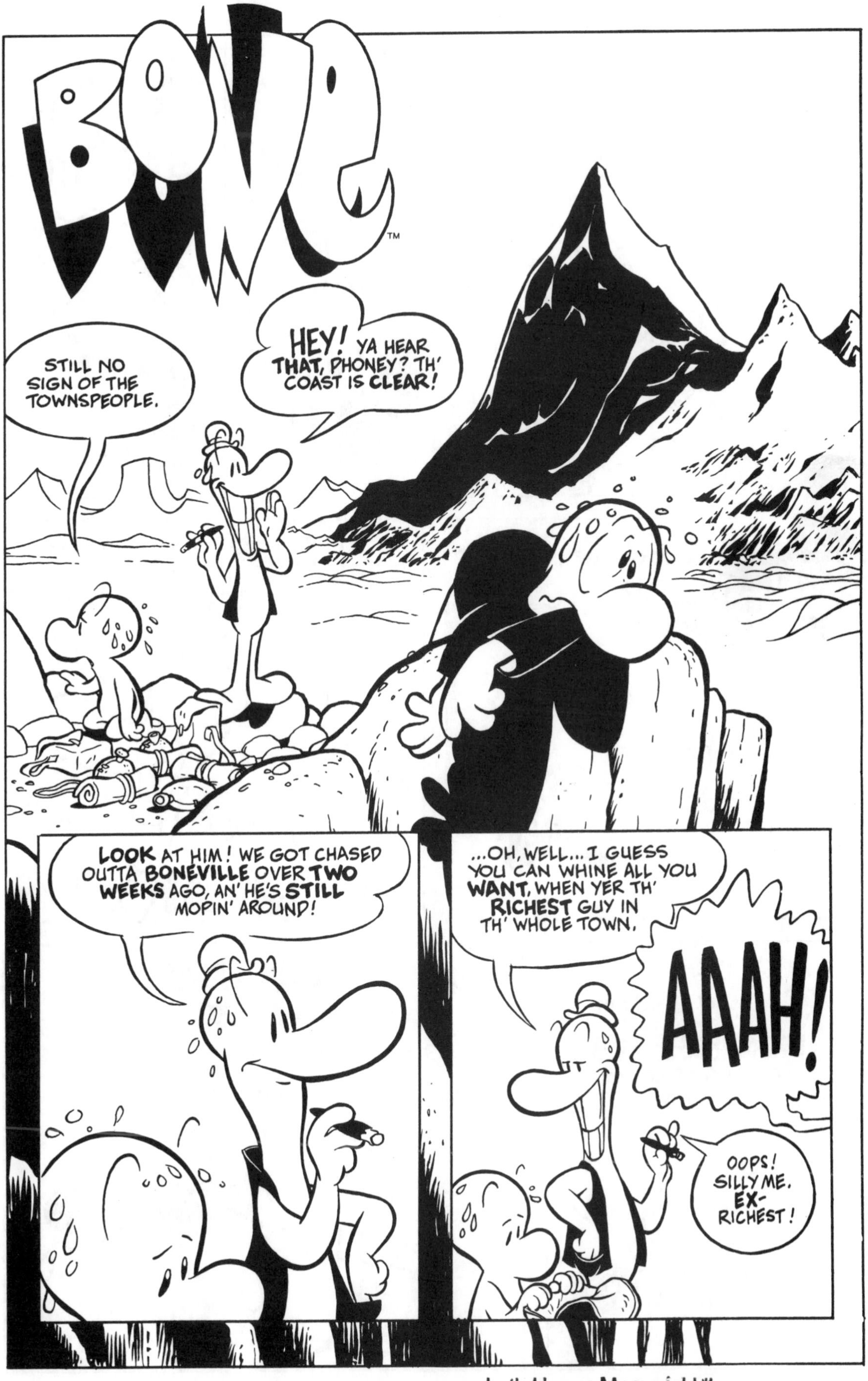
BONE™
STILL NO SIGN OF THE TOWNSPEOPLE.
HEY! YA HEAR THAT, PHONEY? TH' COAST IS CLEAR!
LOOK AT HIM! WE GOT CHASED OUTTA BONEVILLE OVER TWO WEEKS AGO, AN' HE'S STILL MOPIN' AROUND!
...OH, WELL... I GUESS YOU CAN WHINE ALL YOU WANT, WHEN YER TH' RICHEST GUY IN TH' WHOLE TOWN.
AAAH!
OOPS! SILLY ME. EX-RICHEST!

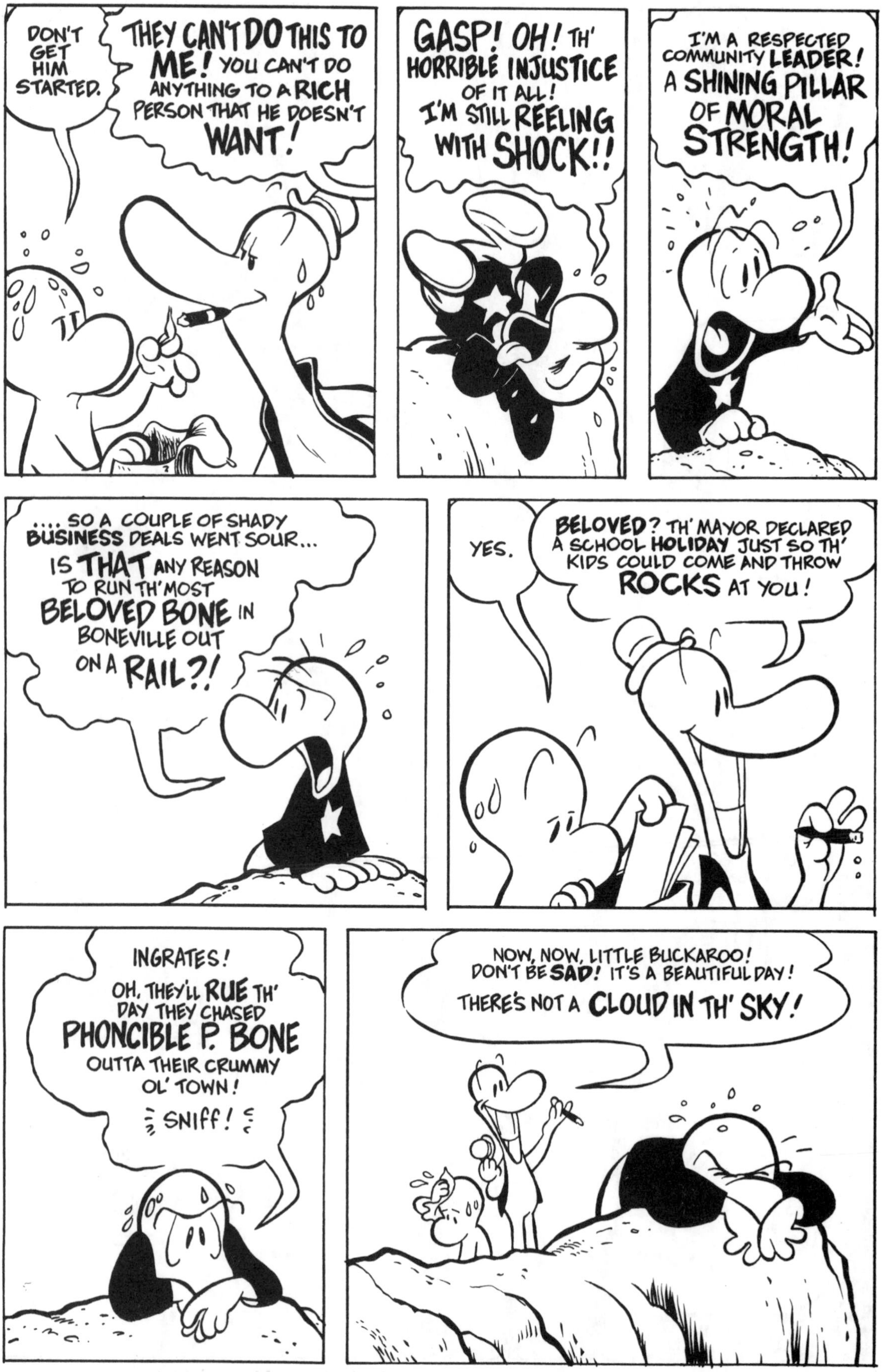
DON'T GET HIM STARTED.
THEY CAN'T DO THIS TO ME! YOU CAN'T DO ANYTHING TO A RICH PERSON THAT HE DOESN'T WANT!
GASP! OH! TH' HORRIBLE INJUSTICE OF IT ALL! I'M STILL REELING WITH SHOCK!!
I'M A RESPECTED COMMUNITY LEADER! A SHINING PILLAR OF MORAL STRENGTH!
.... SO A COUPLE OF SHADY BUSINESS DEALS WENT SOUR... IS THAT ANY REASON TO RUN TH' MOST BELOVED BONE IN BONEVILLE OUT ON A RAIL?!
YES.
BELOVED? TH' MAYOR DECLARED A SCHOOL HOLIDAY JUST SO TH' KIDS COULD COME AND THROW ROCKS AT YOU!
INGRATES! OH, THEY'LL RUE TH' DAY THEY CHASED PHONCIBLE P. BONE OUTTA THEIR CRUMMY OL' TOWN! SNIFF!
NOW, NOW, LITTLE BUCKAROO! DON'T BE SAD! IT'S A BEAUTIFUL DAY! THERE'S NOT A CLOUD IN TH' SKY!

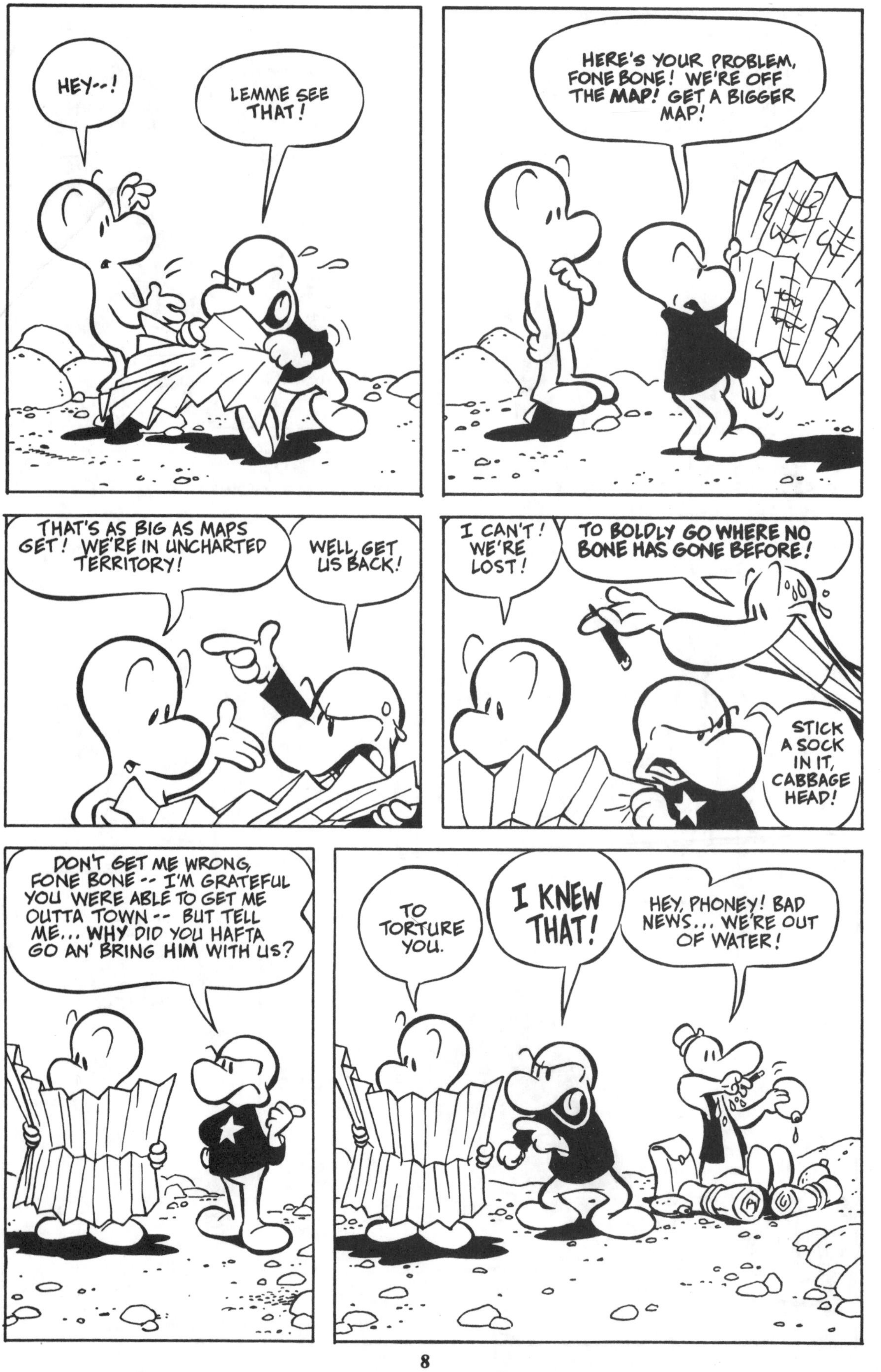
HEY--!
LEMME SEE THAT!
HERE'S YOUR PROBLEM, FONE BONE! WE'RE OFF THE MAP! GET A BIGGER MAP!
THAT'S AS BIG AS MAPS GET! WE'RE IN UNCHARTED TERRITORY!
WELL, GET US BACK!
I CAN'T! WE'RE LOST!
TO BOLDLY GO WHERE NO BONE HAS GONE BEFORE!
STICK A SOCK IN IT, CABBAGE HEAD!
DON'T GET ME WRONG, FONE BONE -- I'M GRATEFUL YOU WERE ABLE TO GET ME OUTTA TOWN -- BUT TELL ME... WHY DID YOU HAFTA GO AN' BRING HIM WITH US?
TO TORTURE YOU.
I KNEW THAT!
HEY, PHONEY! BAD NEWS... WE'RE OUT OF WATER!

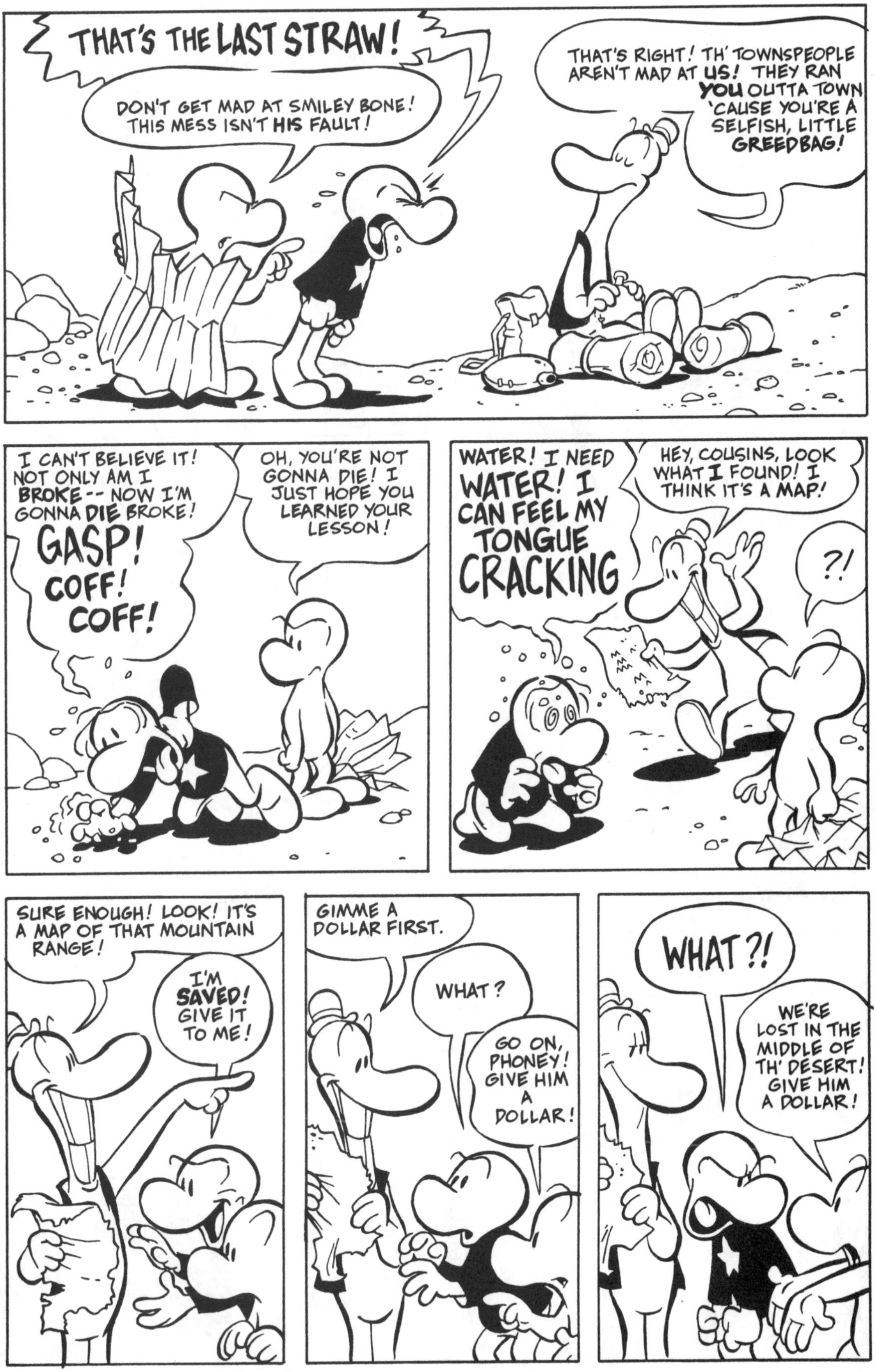

THAT'S THE LAST STRAW!
DON'T GET MAD AT SMILEY BONE! THIS MESS ISN'T HIS FAULT!
THAT'S RIGHT! TH' TOWNSPEOPLE AREN'T MAD AT US! THEY RAN YOU OUTTA TOWN 'CAUSE YOU'RE A SELFISH, LITTLE GREEDBAG!
I CAN'T BELIEVE IT! NOT ONLY AM I BROKE-- NOW I'M GONNA DIE BROKE! GASP! COFF! COFF!
OH, YOU'RE NOT GONNA DIE! I JUST HOPE YOU LEARNED YOUR LESSON!
WATER! I NEED WATER! I CAN FEEL MY TONGUE CRACKING
HEY, COUSINS, LOOK WHAT I FOUND! I THINK IT'S A MAP!
?!
SURE ENOUGH! LOOK! IT'S A MAP OF THAT MOUNTAIN RANGE!
I'M SAVED! GIVE IT TO ME!
GIMME A DOLLAR FIRST.
WHAT?
GO ON, PHONEY! GIVE HIM A DOLLAR!
WHAT?!
WE'RE LOST IN THE MIDDLE OF TH' DESERT! GIVE HIM A DOLLAR!

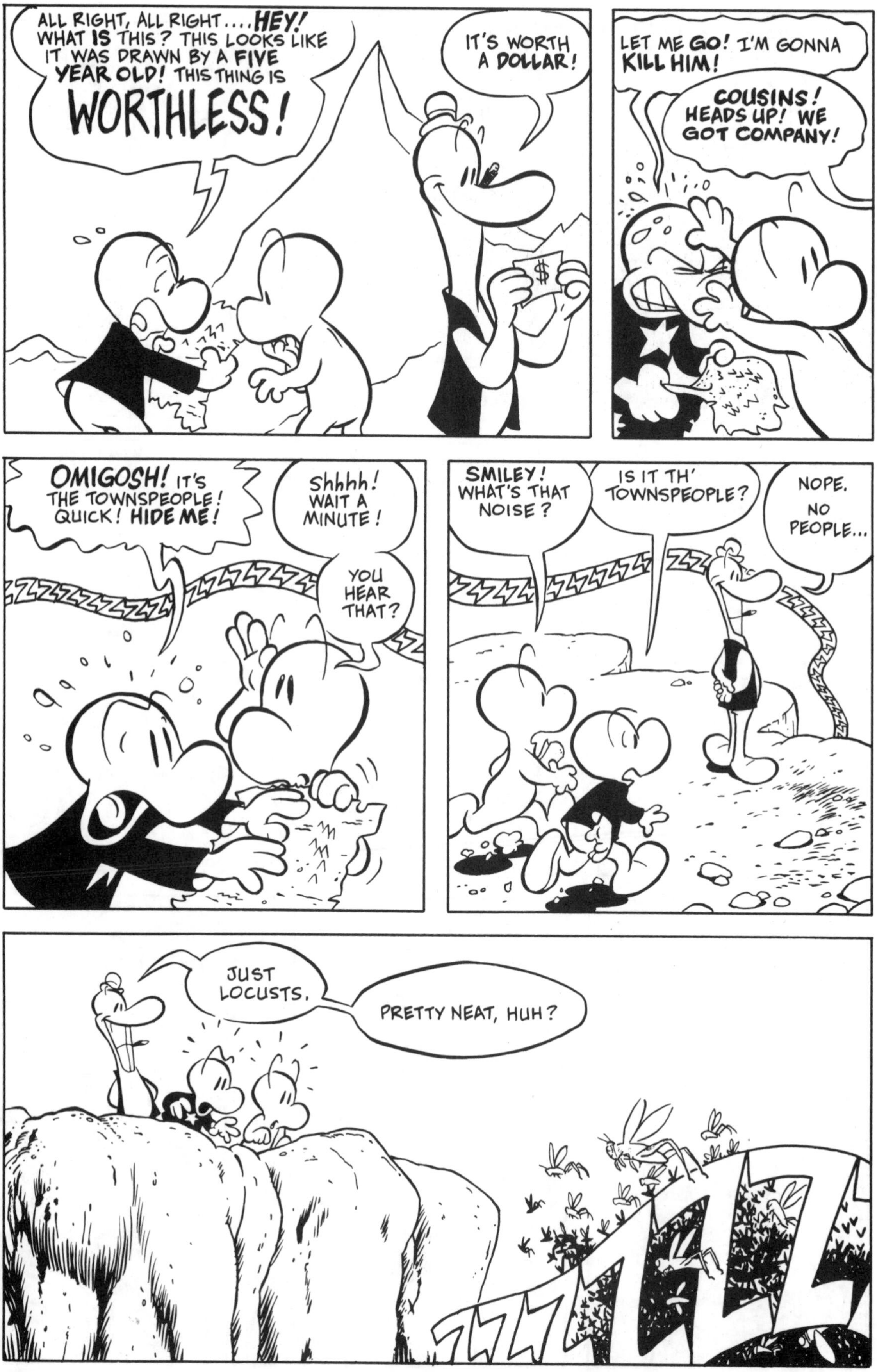
ALL RIGHT, ALL RIGHT.... HEY! WHAT IS THIS? THIS LOOKS LIKE IT WAS DRAWN BY A FIVE YEAR OLD! THIS THING IS WORTHLESS!
IT'S WORTH A DOLLAR!
$
LET ME GO! I'M GONNA KILL HIM!
COUSINS! HEADS UP! WE GOT COMPANY!
OMIGOSH! IT'S THE TOWNSPEOPLE! QUICK! HIDE ME!
Shhhh! WAIT A MINUTE!
YOU HEAR THAT?
SMILEY! WHAT'S THAT NOISE?
IS IT TH' TOWNSPEOPLE?
NOPE. NO PEOPLE...
JUST LOCUSTS.
PRETTY NEAT, HUH?

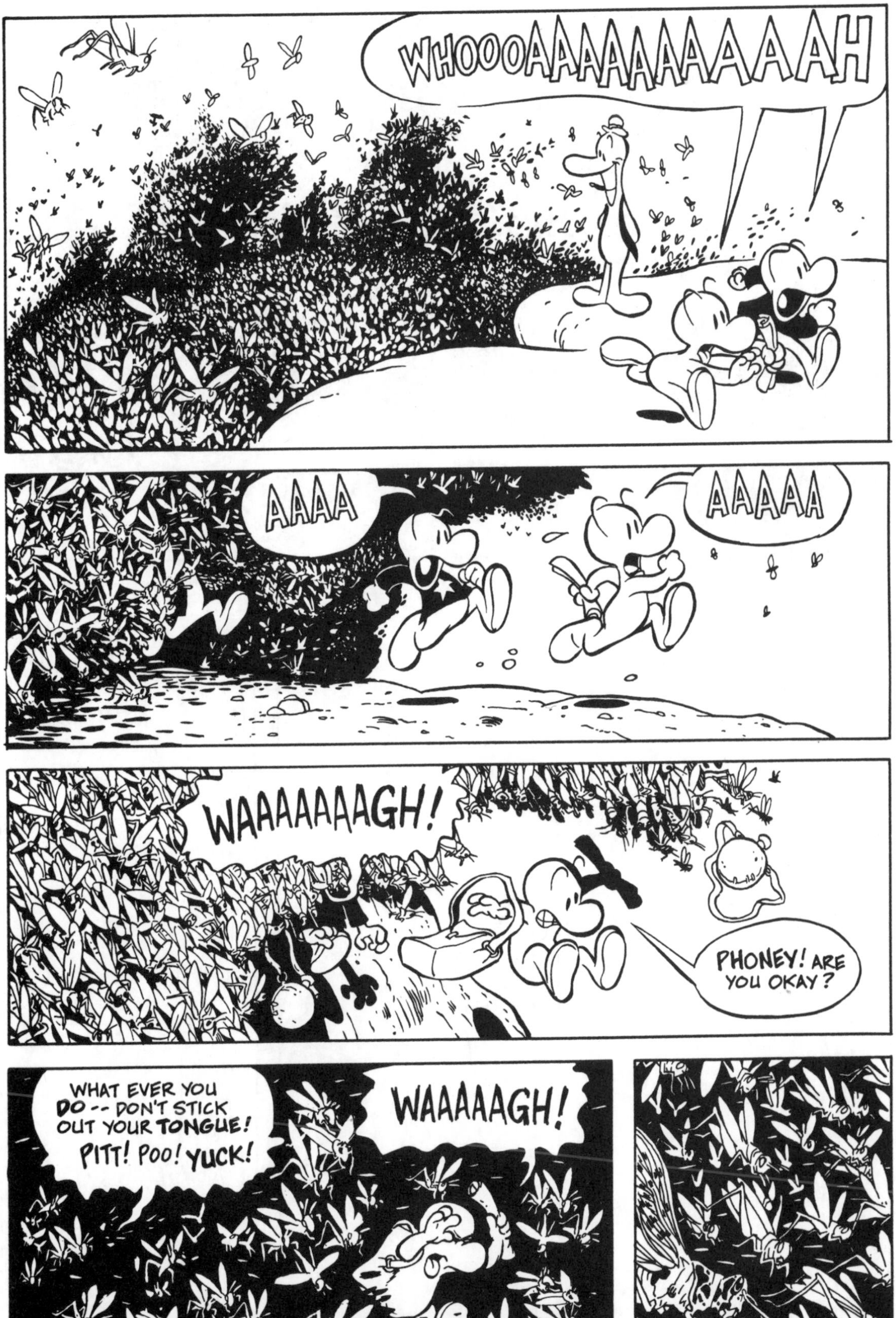
WHOOOAAAAAAAAAAH
AAAA
AAAAA
WAAAAAAAGH!
PHONEY! ARE YOU OKAY?
WHAT EVER YOU DO -- DON'T STICK OUT YOUR TONGUE! PITT! POO! YUCK!
WAAAAGH!

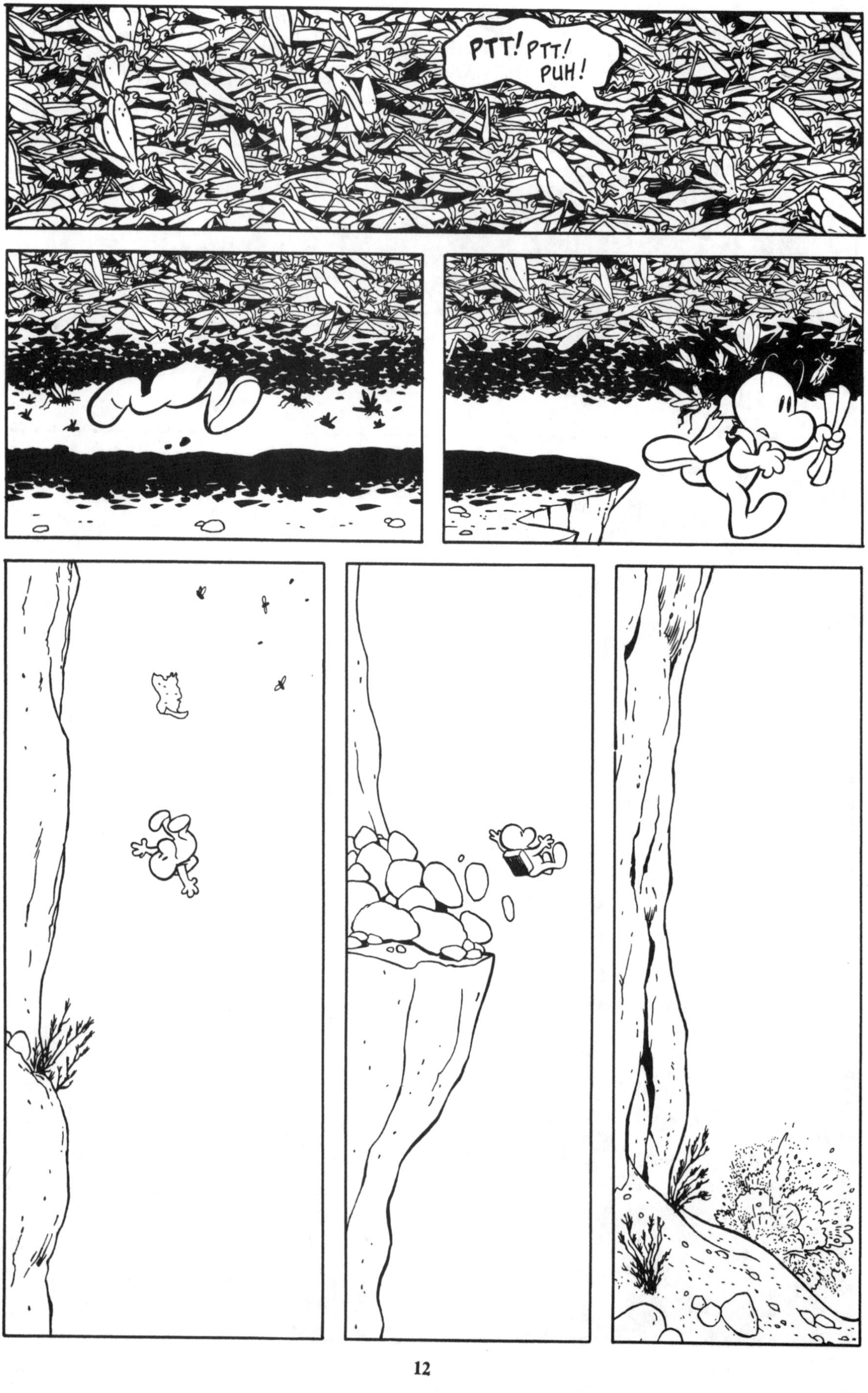
PTT! PTT! PUH!

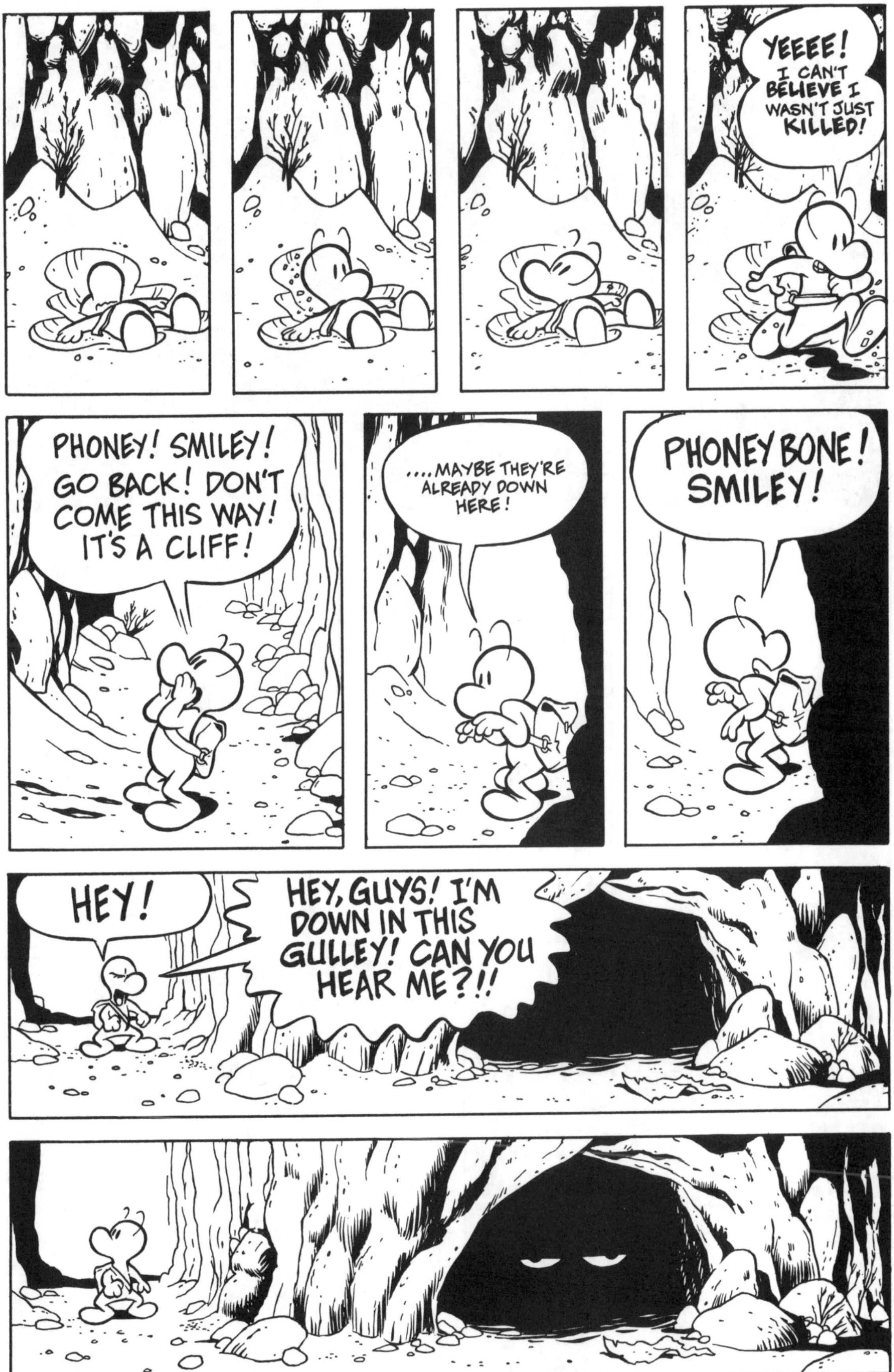
YEEEE! I CAN'T BELIEVE I WASN'T JUST KILLED!
PHONEY! SMILEY! GO BACK! DON'T COME THIS WAY! IT'S A CLIFF!
....MAYBE THEY'RE ALREADY DOWN HERE!
PHONEY BONE! SMILEY!
HEY!
HEY, GUYS! I'M DOWN IN THIS GULLEY! CAN YOU HEAR ME?!!

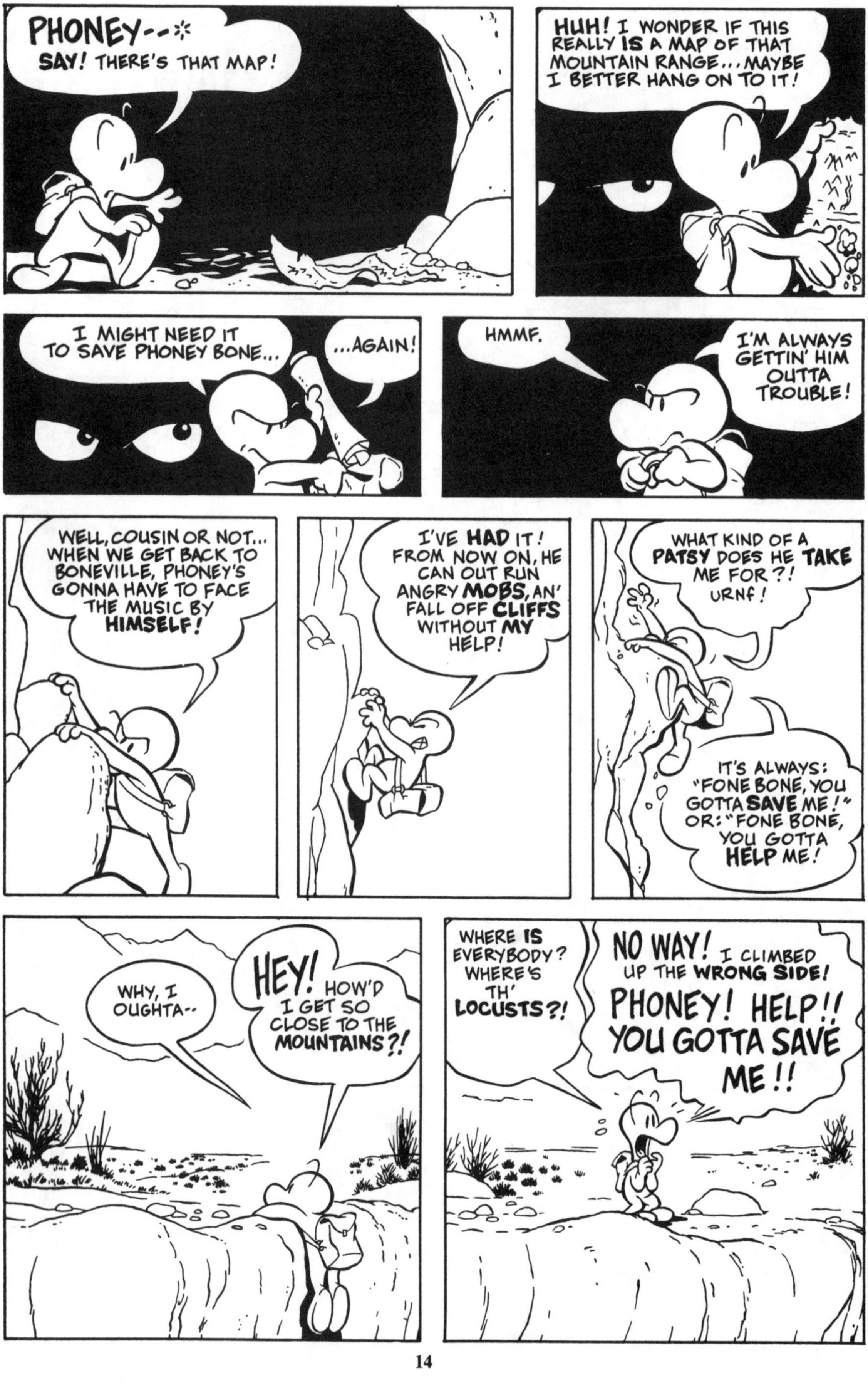

PHONEY--*
SAY! THERE'S THAT MAP!
HUH! I WONDER IF THIS REALLY IS A MAP OF THAT MOUNTAIN RANGE... MAYBE I BETTER HANG ON TO IT!
I MIGHT NEED IT TO SAVE PHONEY BONE...
...AGAIN!
HMMF.
I'M ALWAYS GETTIN' HIM OUTTA TROUBLE!
WELL, COUSIN OR NOT... WHEN WE GET BACK TO BONEVILLE, PHONEY'S GONNA HAVE TO FACE THE MUSIC BY HIMSELF!
I'VE HAD IT! FROM NOW ON, HE CAN OUT RUN ANGRY MOBS, AN' FALL OFF CLIFFS WITHOUT MY HELP!
WHAT KIND OF A PATSY DOES HE TAKE ME FOR?! URNF!
IT'S ALWAYS: "FONE BONE, YOU GOTTA SAVE ME!" OR: "FONE BONE, YOU GOTTA HELP ME!
WHY, I OUGHTA--
HEY! HOW'D I GET SO CLOSE TO THE MOUNTAINS?!
WHERE IS EVERYBODY? WHERE'S TH' LOCUSTS?!
NO WAY! I CLIMBED UP THE WRONG SIDE! PHONEY! HELP!! YOU GOTTA SAVE ME!!

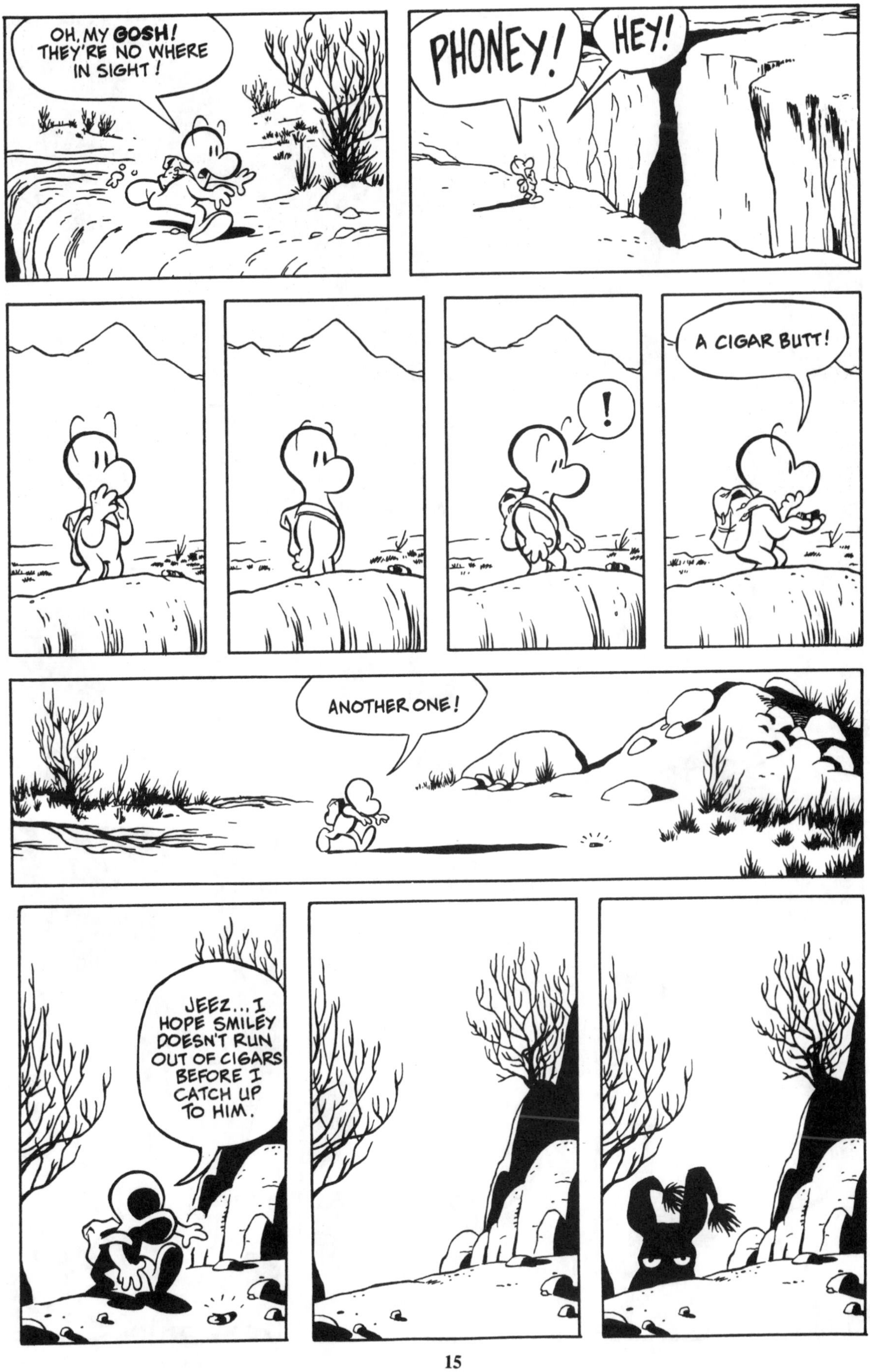
OH, MY GOSH! THEY'RE NO WHERE IN SIGHT!
PHONEY!
HEY!
!
A CIGAR BUTT!
ANOTHER ONE!
JEEZ... I HOPE SMILEY DOESN'T RUN OUT OF CIGARS BEFORE I CATCH UP TO HIM.

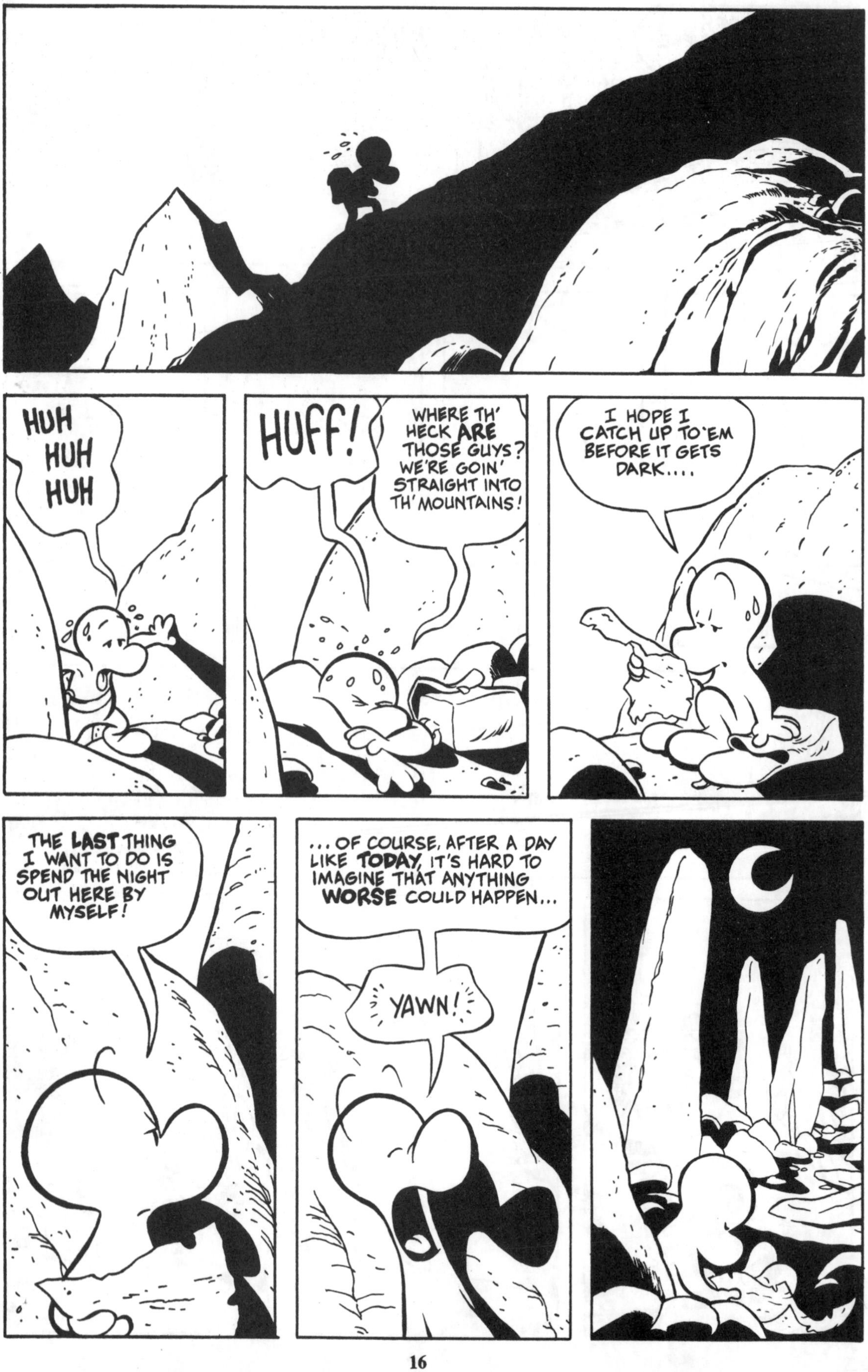

HUH HUH HUH
HUFF!
WHERE TH' HECK ARE THOSE GUYS? WE'RE GOIN' STRAIGHT INTO TH' MOUNTAINS!
I HOPE I CATCH UP TO 'EM BEFORE IT GETS DARK....
THE LAST THING I WANT TO DO IS SPEND THE NIGHT OUT HERE BY MYSELF!
...OF COURSE, AFTER A DAY LIKE TODAY, IT'S HARD TO IMAGINE THAT ANYTHING WORSE COULD HAPPEN...
YAWN!

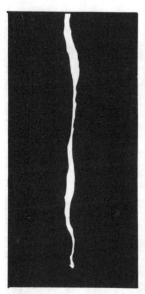

OOG.... I MUST'VE FALLEN ASLEEP.

WHERE AM I?

YOU AWAKE?

HUH? WHO'S THERE?

YOU GOT A LIGHT?

SMILEY? IS THAT YOU?

OH, *BOY*, AM I GLAD TO SEE *YOU*! HOLD ON, I'VE GOT A MATCH IN MY BAG, HERE!

SKRITCH

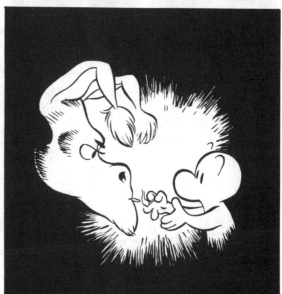

AAAH!

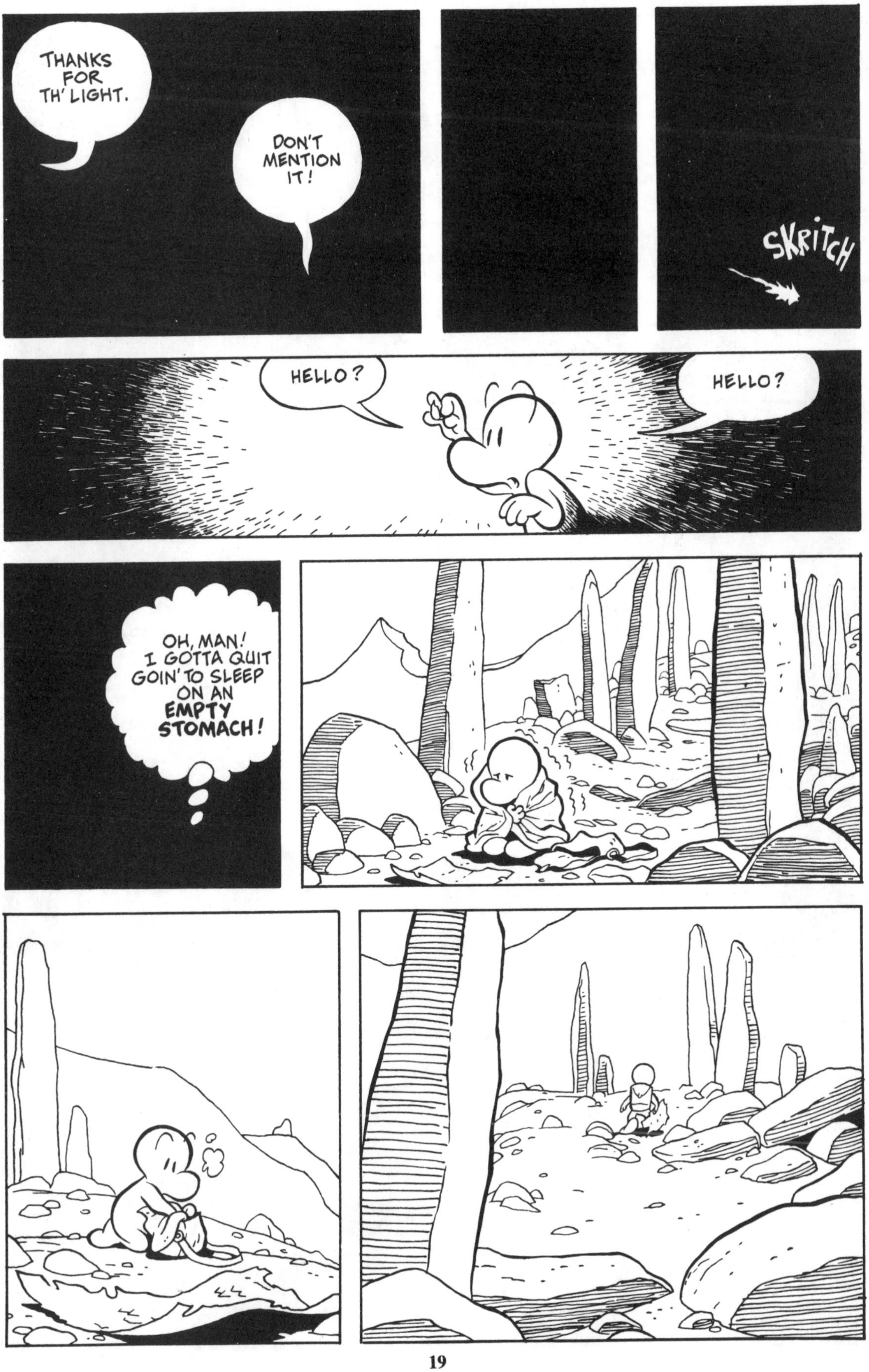
THANKS FOR TH' LIGHT.
DON'T MENTION IT!
SKRITCH
HELLO?
HELLO?
OH, MAN! I GOTTA QUIT GOIN' TO SLEEP ON AN EMPTY STOMACH!

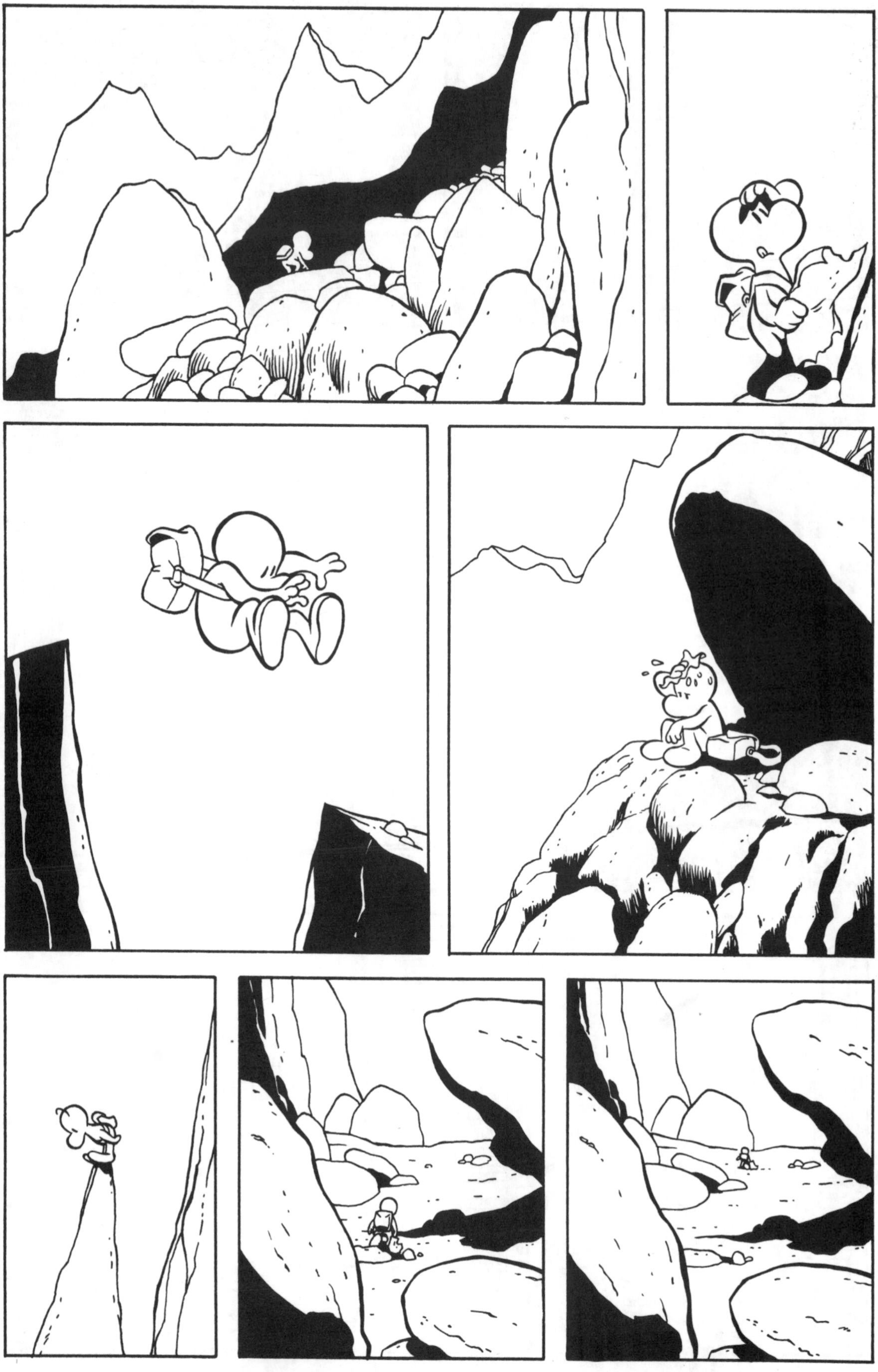

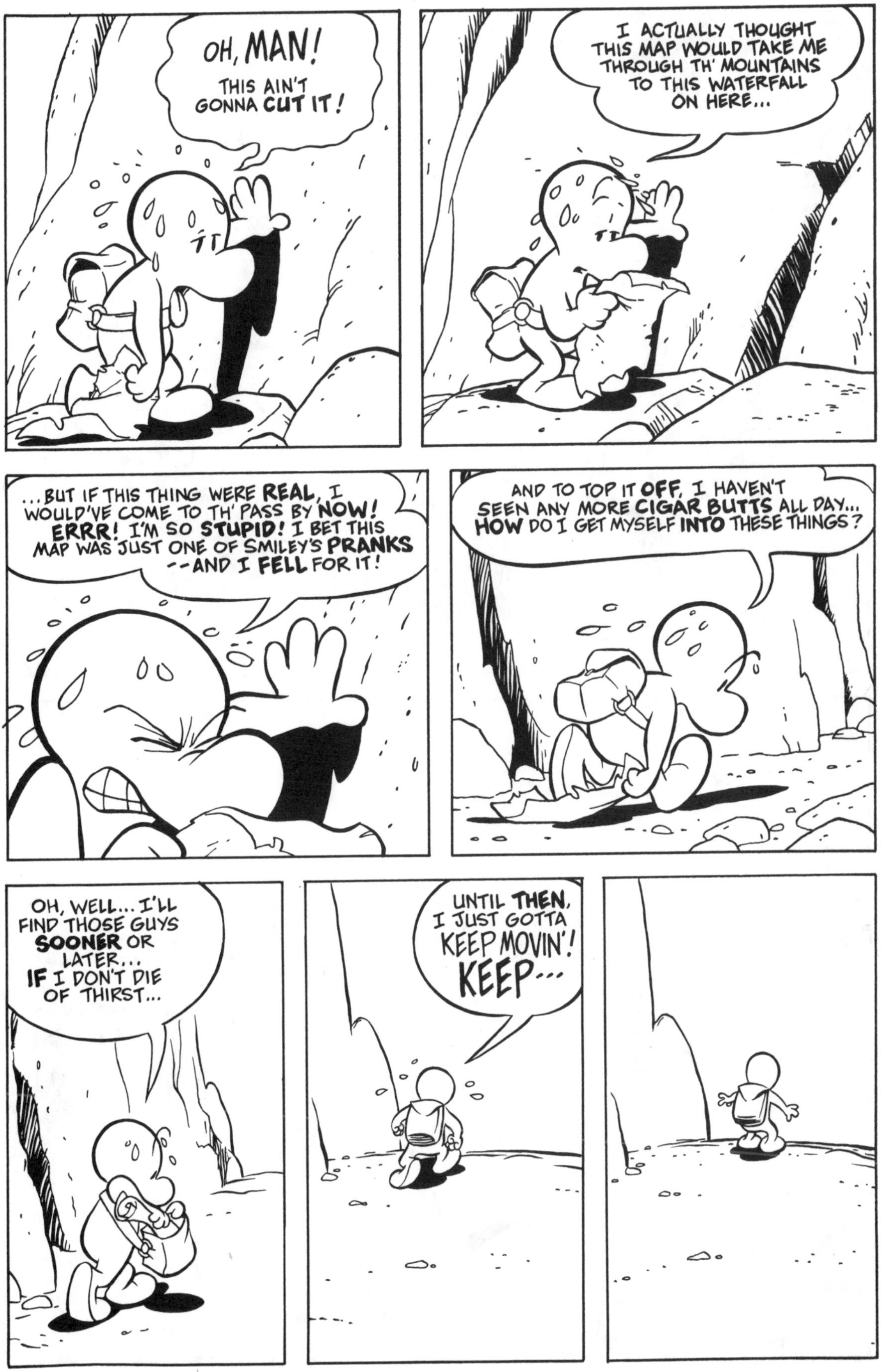
OH, MAN! THIS AIN'T GONNA CUT IT!
I ACTUALLY THOUGHT THIS MAP WOULD TAKE ME THROUGH TH' MOUNTAINS TO THIS WATERFALL ON HERE...
...BUT IF THIS THING WERE REAL, I WOULD'VE COME TO TH' PASS BY NOW! ERRR! I'M SO STUPID! I BET THIS MAP WAS JUST ONE OF SMILEY'S PRANKS --AND I FELL FOR IT!
AND TO TOP IT OFF, I HAVEN'T SEEN ANY MORE CIGAR BUTTS ALL DAY... HOW DO I GET MYSELF INTO THESE THINGS?
OH, WELL... I'LL FIND THOSE GUYS SOONER OR LATER... IF I DON'T DIE OF THIRST...
UNTIL THEN, I JUST GOTTA KEEP MOVIN'! KEEP...

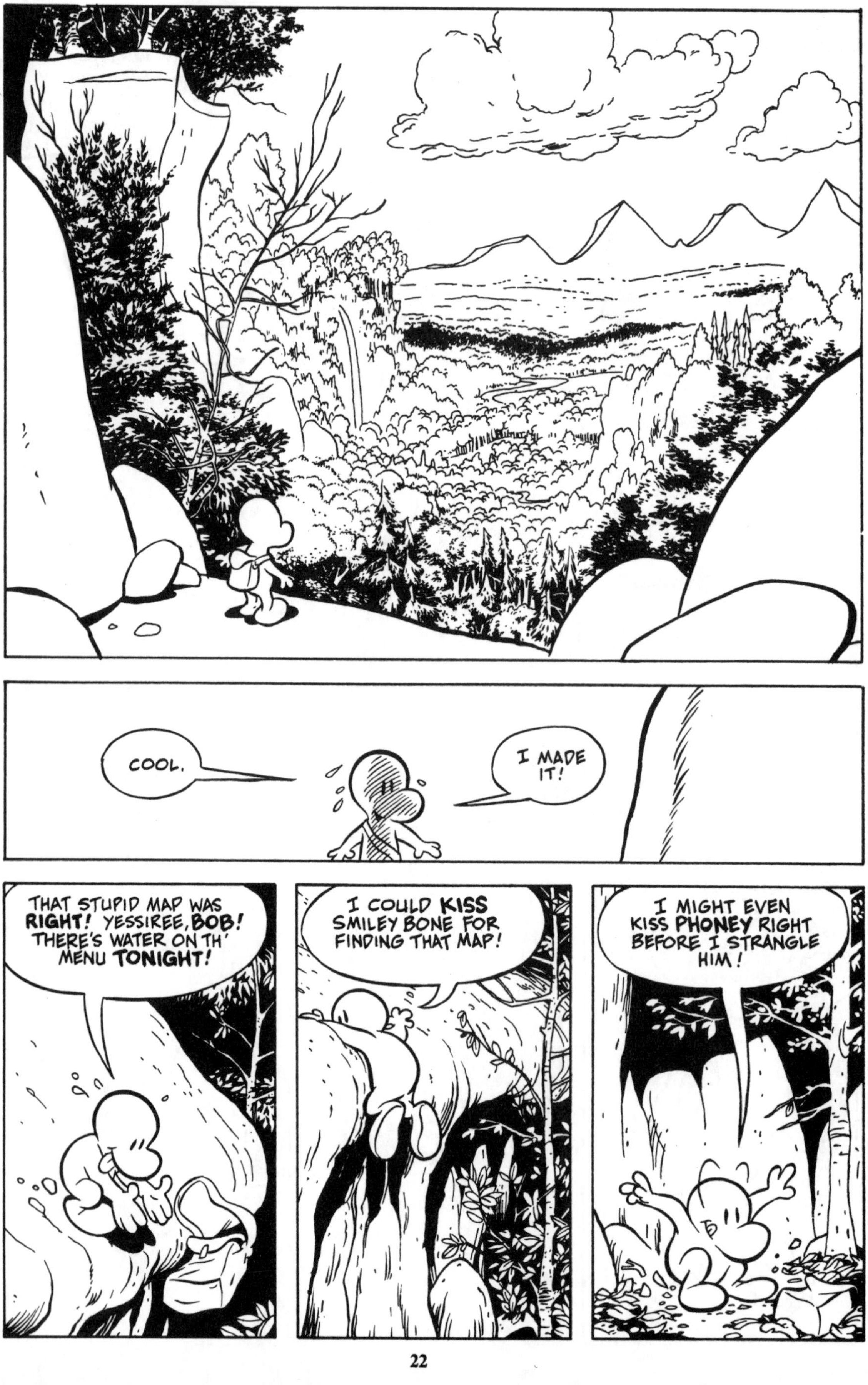
COOL.
I MADE IT!
THAT STUPID MAP WAS **RIGHT**! YESSIREE, **BOB**! THERE'S WATER ON TH' MENU **TONIGHT**!
I COULD **KISS** SMILEY BONE FOR FINDING THAT MAP!
I MIGHT EVEN KISS **PHONEY** RIGHT BEFORE I STRANGLE HIM!

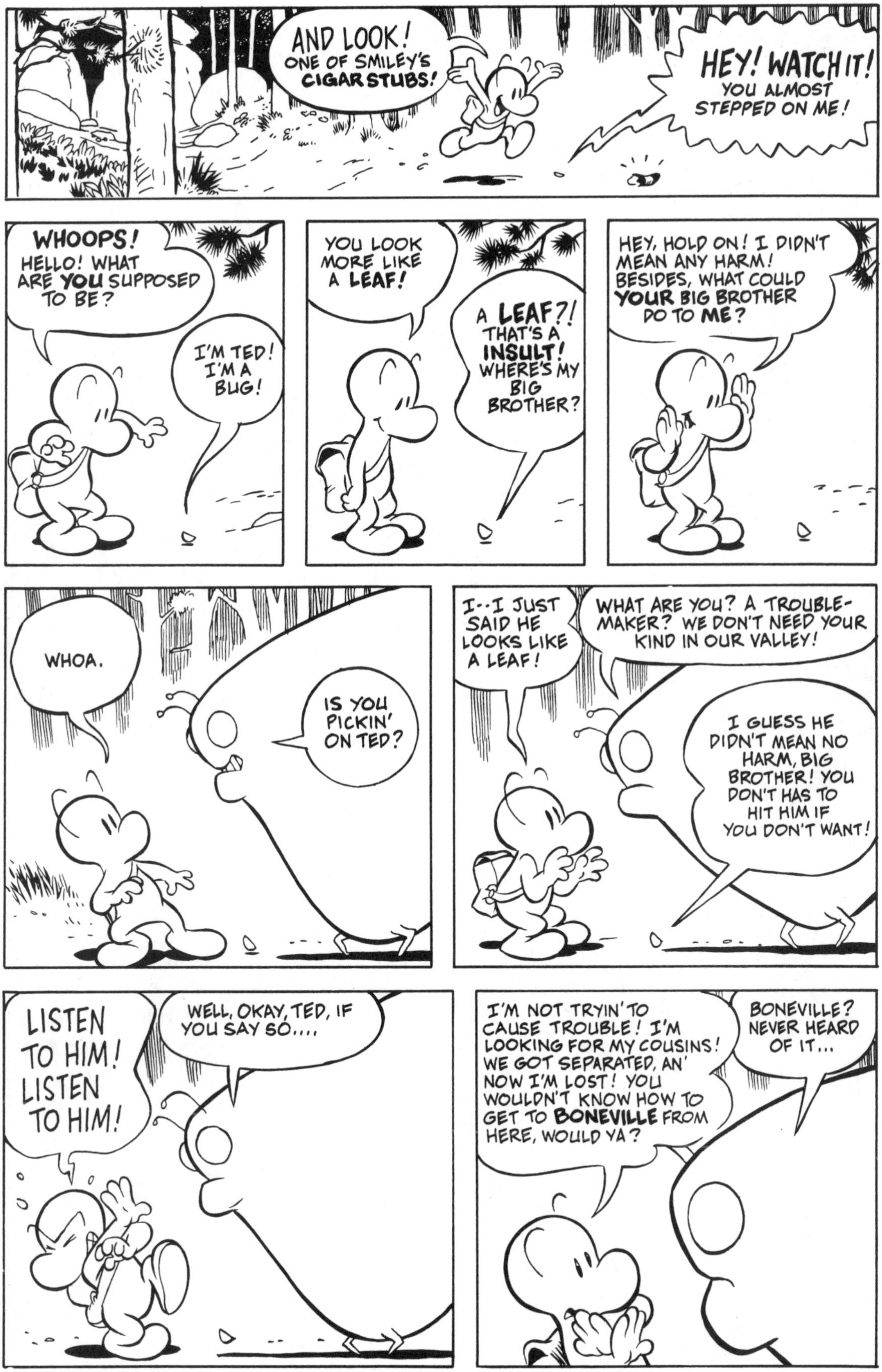
AND LOOK! ONE OF SMILEY'S CIGAR STUBS!
HEY! WATCH IT! YOU ALMOST STEPPED ON ME!
WHOOPS! HELLO! WHAT ARE YOU SUPPOSED TO BE?
I'M TED! I'M A BUG!
YOU LOOK MORE LIKE A LEAF!
A LEAF?! THAT'S A INSULT! WHERE'S MY BIG BROTHER?
HEY, HOLD ON! I DIDN'T MEAN ANY HARM! BESIDES, WHAT COULD YOUR BIG BROTHER DO TO ME?
WHOA.
IS YOU PICKIN' ON TED?
I--I JUST SAID HE LOOKS LIKE A LEAF!
WHAT ARE YOU? A TROUBLE-MAKER? WE DON'T NEED YOUR KIND IN OUR VALLEY!
I GUESS HE DIDN'T MEAN NO HARM, BIG BROTHER! YOU DON'T HAS TO HIT HIM IF YOU DON'T WANT!
LISTEN TO HIM! LISTEN TO HIM!
WELL, OKAY, TED, IF YOU SAY SO....
I'M NOT TRYIN' TO CAUSE TROUBLE! I'M LOOKING FOR MY COUSINS! WE GOT SEPARATED, AN' NOW I'M LOST! YOU WOULDN'T KNOW HOW TO GET TO BONEVILLE FROM HERE, WOULD YA?
BONEVILLE? NEVER HEARD OF IT...

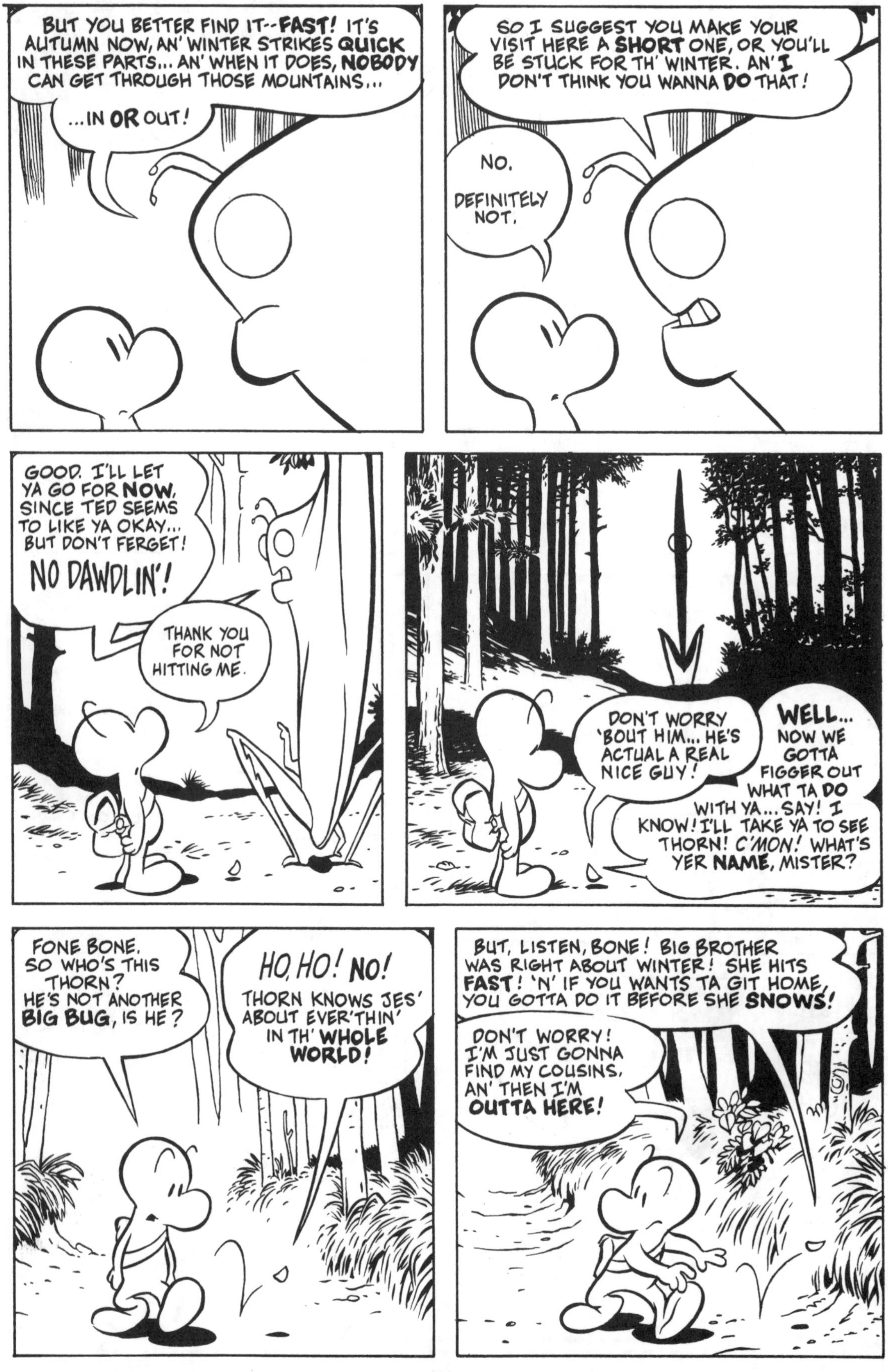
BUT YOU BETTER FIND IT--FAST! IT'S AUTUMN NOW, AN' WINTER STRIKES QUICK IN THESE PARTS... AN' WHEN IT DOES, NOBODY CAN GET THROUGH THOSE MOUNTAINS...
...IN OR OUT!
SO I SUGGEST YOU MAKE YOUR VISIT HERE A SHORT ONE, OR YOU'LL BE STUCK FOR TH' WINTER. AN' I DON'T THINK YOU WANNA DO THAT!
NO. DEFINITELY NOT.
GOOD. I'LL LET YA GO FOR NOW, SINCE TED SEEMS TO LIKE YA OKAY... BUT DON'T FERGET! NO DAWDLIN'!
THANK YOU FOR NOT HITTING ME.
DON'T WORRY 'BOUT HIM... HE'S ACTUAL A REAL NICE GUY!
WELL... NOW WE GOTTA FIGGER OUT WHAT TA DO WITH YA... SAY! I KNOW! I'LL TAKE YA TO SEE THORN! C'MON! WHAT'S YER NAME, MISTER?
FONE BONE. SO WHO'S THIS THORN? HE'S NOT ANOTHER BIG BUG, IS HE?
HO, HO! NO! THORN KNOWS JES' ABOUT EVER'THIN' IN TH' WHOLE WORLD!
BUT, LISTEN, BONE! BIG BROTHER WAS RIGHT ABOUT WINTER! SHE HITS FAST! 'N' IF YOU WANTS TA GIT HOME, YOU GOTTA DO IT BEFORE SHE SNOWS!
DON'T WORRY! I'M JUST GONNA FIND MY COUSINS, AN' THEN I'M OUTTA HERE!

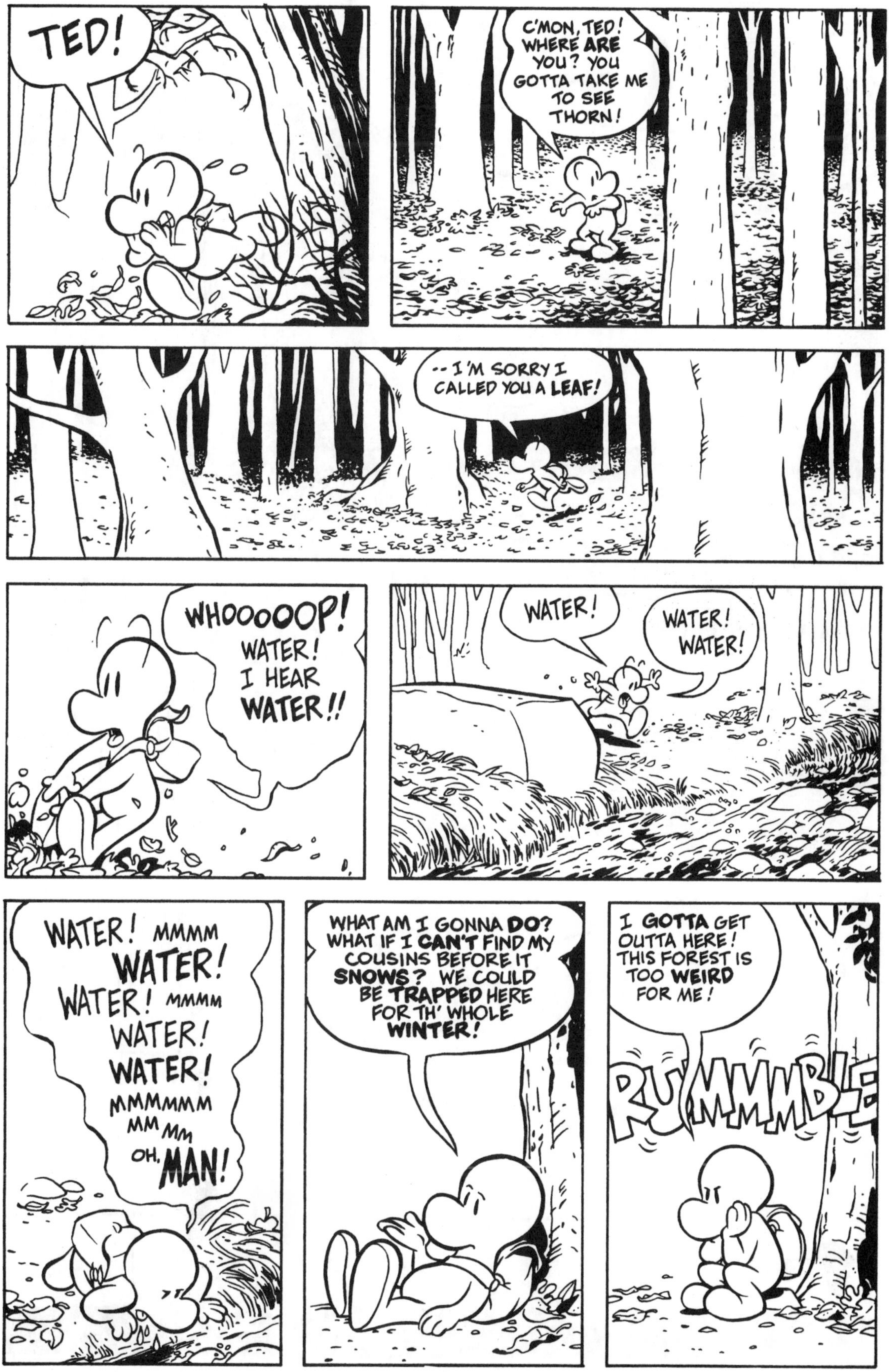
TED!
C'MON, TED! WHERE ARE YOU? YOU GOTTA TAKE ME TO SEE THORN!
-- I'M SORRY I CALLED YOU A LEAF!
WHOOOOOP! WATER! I HEAR WATER!!
WATER!
WATER! WATER!
WATER! MMMM WATER! WATER! MMMM WATER! WATER! MMMMMM MM MM OH, MAN!
WHAT AM I GONNA DO? WHAT IF I CAN'T FIND MY COUSINS BEFORE IT SNOWS? WE COULD BE TRAPPED HERE FOR TH' WHOLE WINTER!
I GOTTA GET OUTTA HERE! THIS FOREST IS TOO WEIRD FOR ME!
RUMMMMBLE

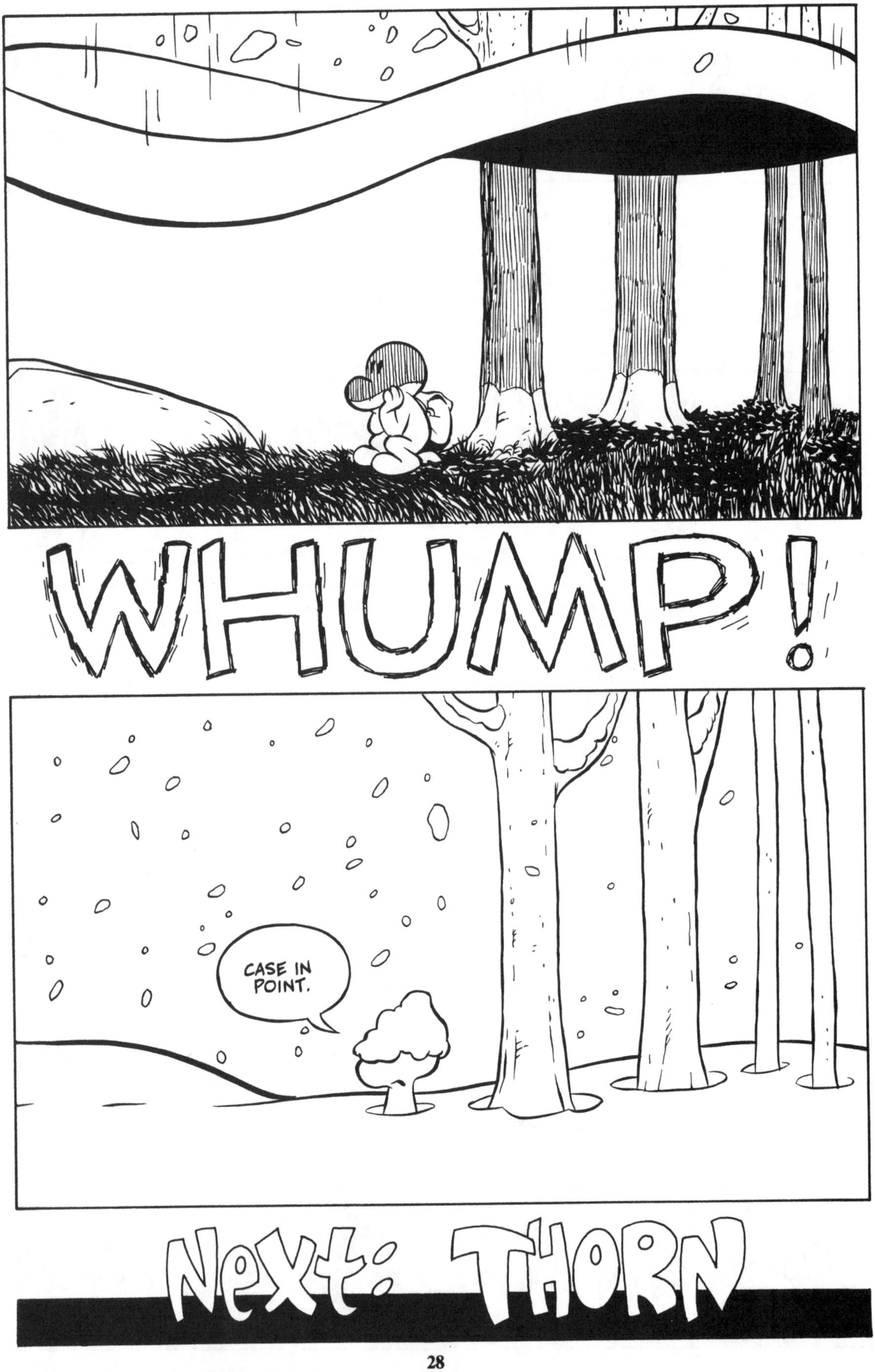
WHUMP!
CASE IN POINT.
NEXT: THORN

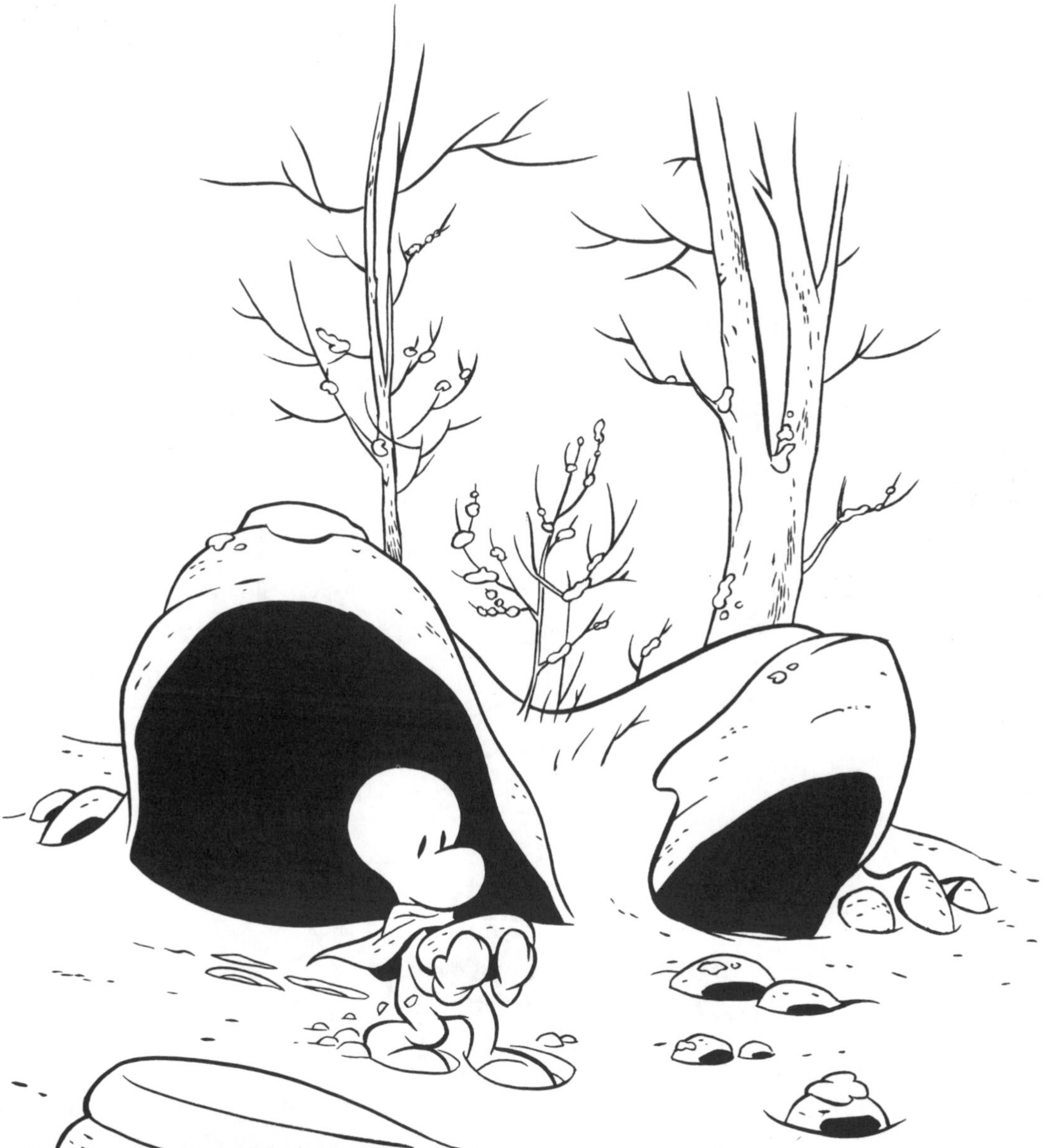

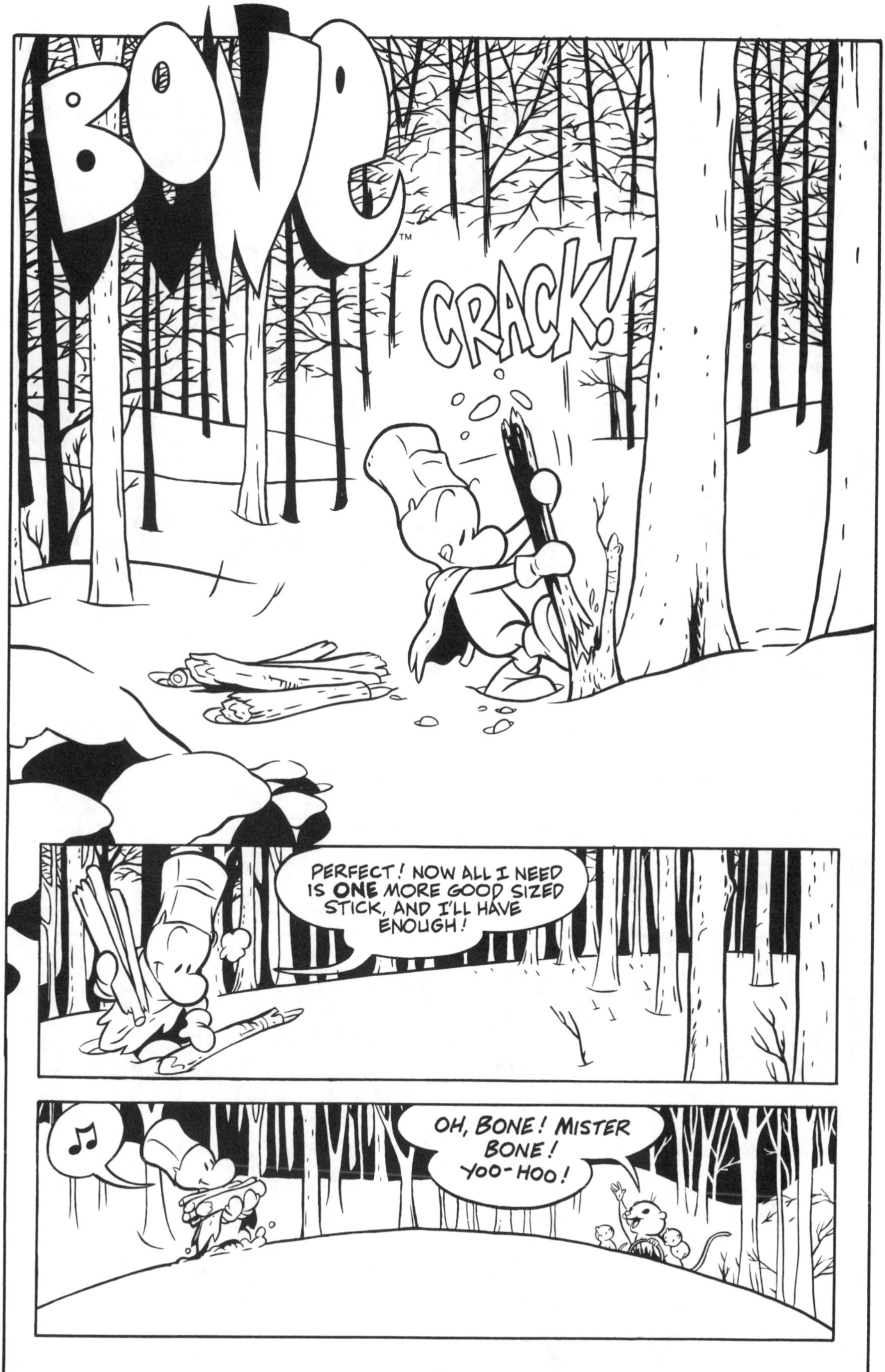
BONE™
CRACK!
PERFECT! NOW ALL I NEED IS ONE MORE GOOD SIZED STICK, AND I'LL HAVE ENOUGH!
♫
OH, BONE! MISTER BONE! YOO-HOO!

HELLO, MIZ 'POSSUM! I HAVEN'T SEEN **YOU** IN A COUPLE OF MONTHS!

OH, I DON'T GET OUT OF TH' HOUSE MUCH IN **WINTER**... 'SPECIALLY WITH **YOUNGUNS!**

THESE CAN'T BE **YOUR** KIDS! THEY'RE ALL GROWN UP!

WELL, IT'S ALMOST **SPRING!** THEY SHOOT UP **FAST** THIS TIME OF YEAR! YOU BOYS REMEMBER FONE BONE?

SURE!

YEAH!

HOW YOU GUYS DOIN'?

WE'RE COOL.

WHERE'D YA GET TH' **HAT?**

YOUR MOM MADE IT FOR ME!

PRETTY DORKY!

MOM BROUGHT YA SOME MORE **BLANKETS** 'N STUFF!

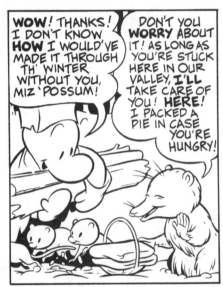

WOW! THANKS! I DON'T KNOW **HOW** I WOULD'VE MADE IT THROUGH TH' WINTER WITHOUT YOU, MIZ 'POSSUM!

DON'T YOU **WORRY** ABOUT IT! AS LONG AS YOU'RE STUCK HERE IN OUR VALLEY, **I'LL** TAKE CARE OF YOU! **HERE!** I PACKED A PIE IN CASE YOU'RE HUNGRY!

DID YOU EVER FIND THOSE COUSINS OF YOURS?

NO, NOT YET. HAVE YOU SEEN **TED** SINCE I TALKED TO YOU LAST?

NOPE. DON'T KNOW MUCH ABOUT WHAT BUGS **DO** IN TH' WINTER, BUT I HAVEN'T SEEN WING **NOR** ANTENNEA OF TED SINCE TH' **SNOW** HIT....

SAY.... WASN'T THERE SOMEONE **ELSE** YOU WANTED ME TO FIND OUT ABOUT?

TED WAS GONNA TAKE ME TO SEE SOMEONE NAMED **THORN.**

OH, THAT'S **RIGHT!** NOPE, HAVEN'T FOUND OUT A **THING!** YOU SURE YOU HAVE ENOUGH BLANKETS?

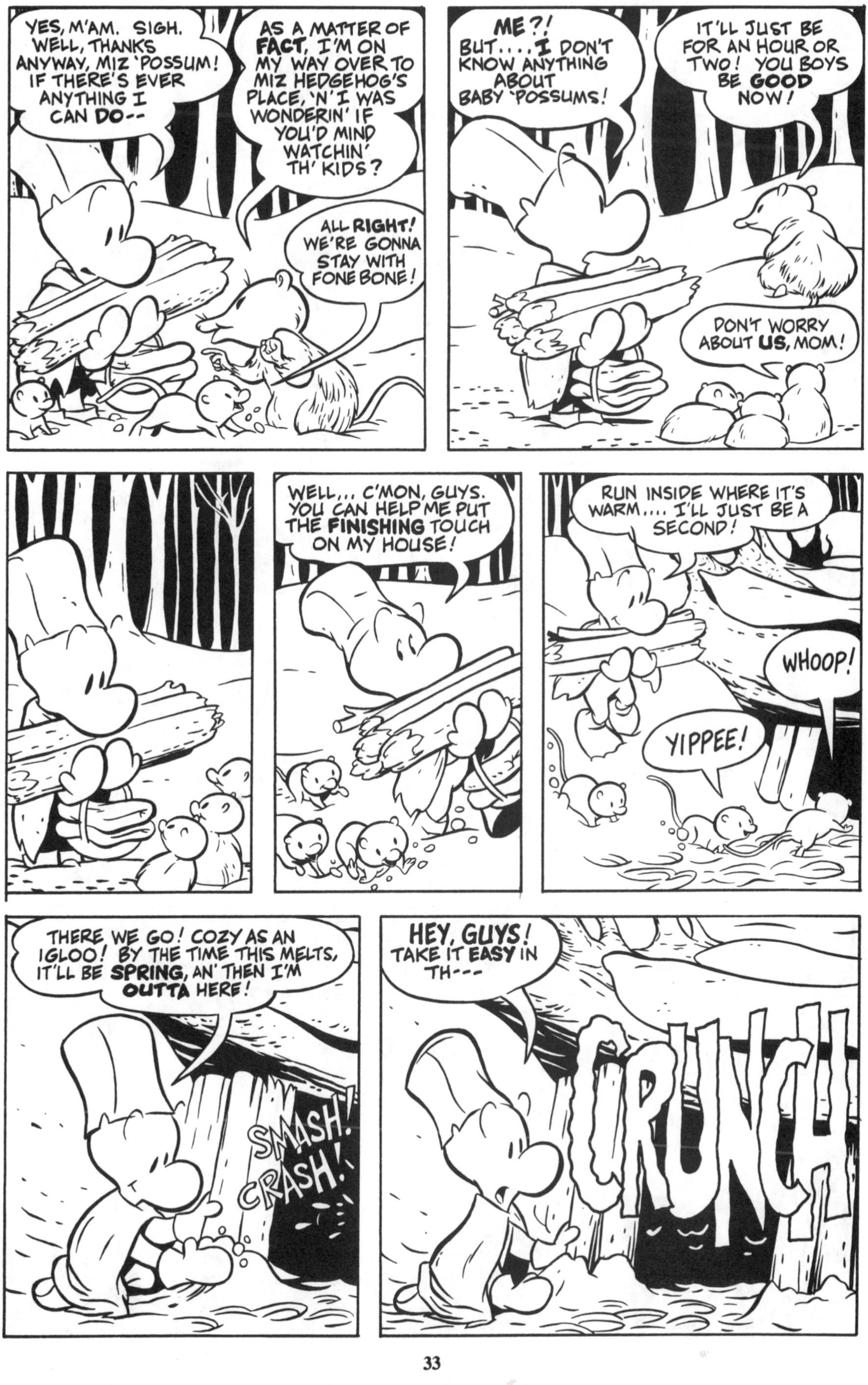
YES, M'AM. SIGH. WELL, THANKS ANYWAY, MIZ 'POSSUM! IF THERE'S EVER ANYTHING I CAN DO--
AS A MATTER OF FACT, I'M ON MY WAY OVER TO MIZ HEDGEHOG'S PLACE, 'N' I WAS WONDERIN' IF YOU'D MIND WATCHIN' TH' KIDS?
ALL RIGHT! WE'RE GONNA STAY WITH FONE BONE!
ME?! BUT.... I DON'T KNOW ANYTHING ABOUT BABY 'POSSUMS!
IT'LL JUST BE FOR AN HOUR OR TWO! YOU BOYS BE GOOD NOW!
DON'T WORRY ABOUT US, MOM!
WELL,.. C'MON, GUYS. YOU CAN HELP ME PUT THE FINISHING TOUCH ON MY HOUSE!
RUN INSIDE WHERE IT'S WARM.... I'LL JUST BE A SECOND!
WHOOP!
YIPPEE!
THERE WE GO! COZY AS AN IGLOO! BY THE TIME THIS MELTS, IT'LL BE SPRING, AN' THEN I'M OUTTA HERE!
SMASH!
CRASH!
HEY, GUYS! TAKE IT EASY IN TH---
CRUNCH

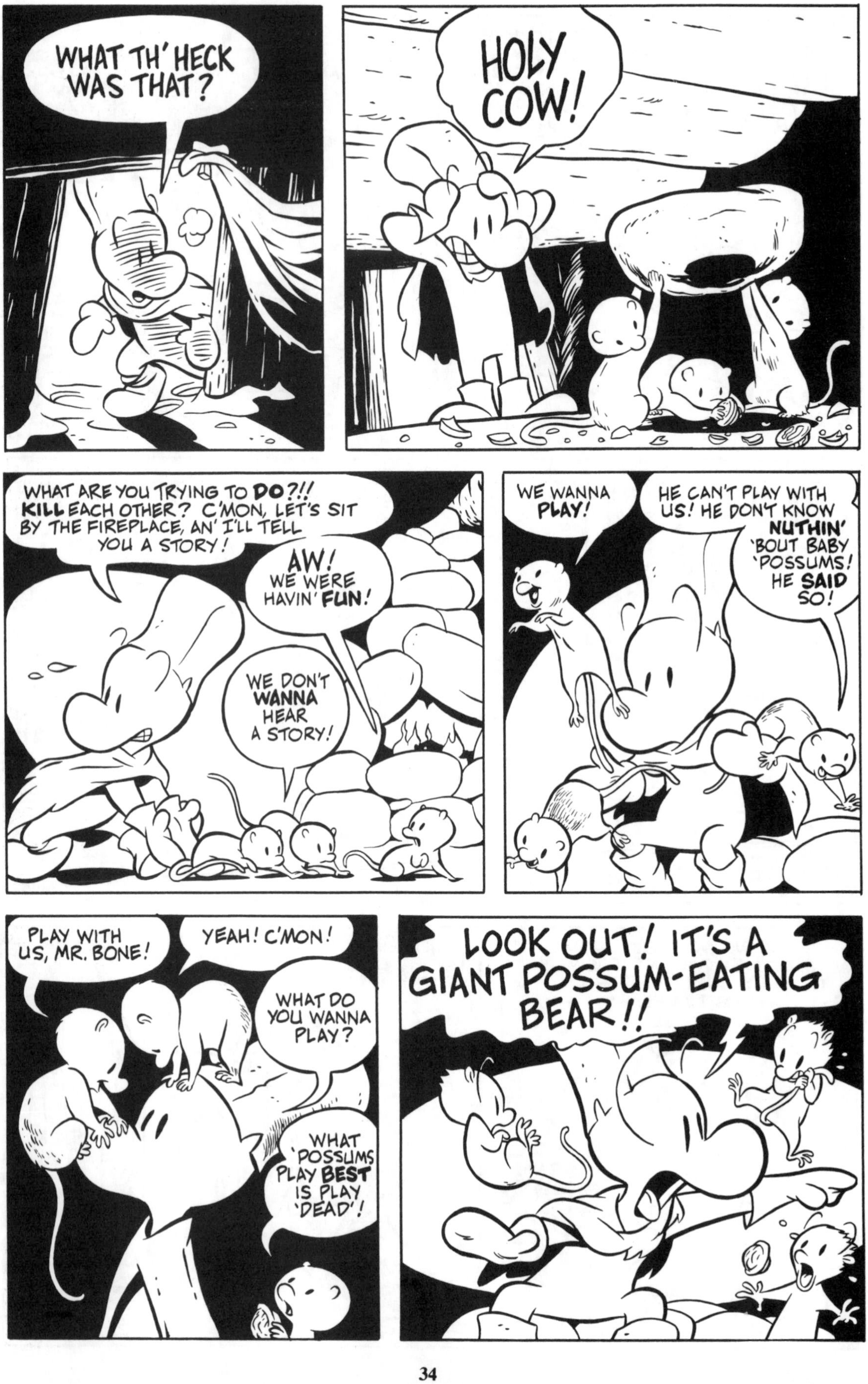
WHAT TH' HECK WAS THAT?
HOLY COW!
WHAT ARE YOU TRYING TO **DO**?!! **KILL** EACH OTHER? C'MON, LET'S SIT BY THE FIREPLACE, AN' I'LL TELL YOU A STORY!
AW! WE WERE HAVIN' **FUN**!
WE DON'T **WANNA** HEAR A STORY!
WE WANNA **PLAY**!
HE CAN'T PLAY WITH US! HE DON'T KNOW **NUTHIN'** 'BOUT BABY 'POSSUMS! HE **SAID** SO!
PLAY WITH US, MR. BONE!
YEAH! C'MON!
WHAT DO YOU WANNA PLAY?
WHAT 'POSSUMS PLAY **BEST** IS PLAY 'DEAD'!
LOOK OUT! IT'S A GIANT POSSUM-EATING BEAR!!

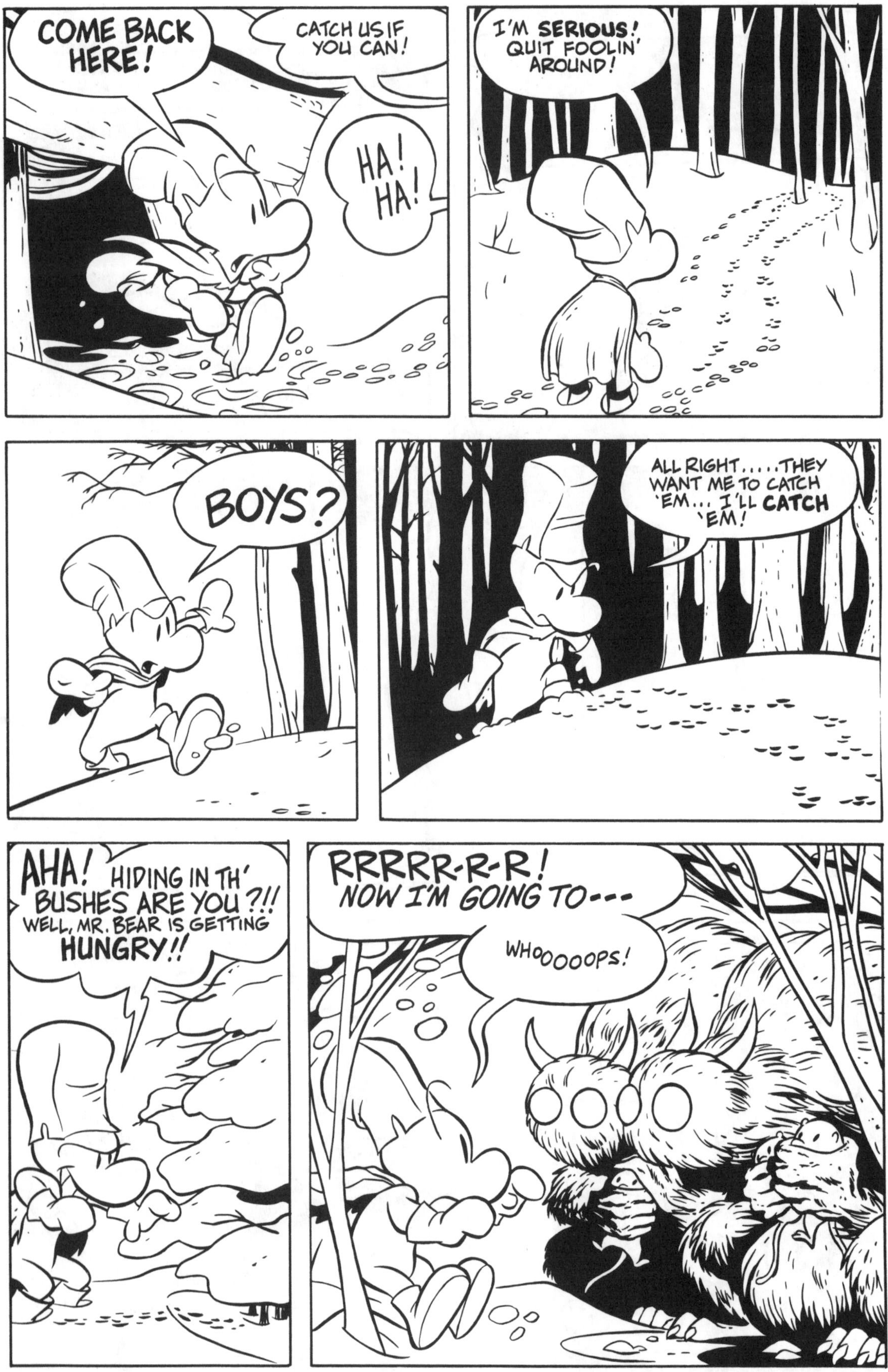
COME BACK HERE!
CATCH US IF YOU CAN!
HA! HA!
I'M **SERIOUS**! QUIT FOOLIN' AROUND!
BOYS?
ALL RIGHT.....THEY WANT ME TO CATCH 'EM... I'LL **CATCH** 'EM!
AHA! HIDING IN TH' BUSHES ARE YOU?!! WELL, MR. BEAR IS GETTING **HUNGRY**!!
RRRRR-R-R! NOW I'M GOING TO---
WHOOOOOPS!

37

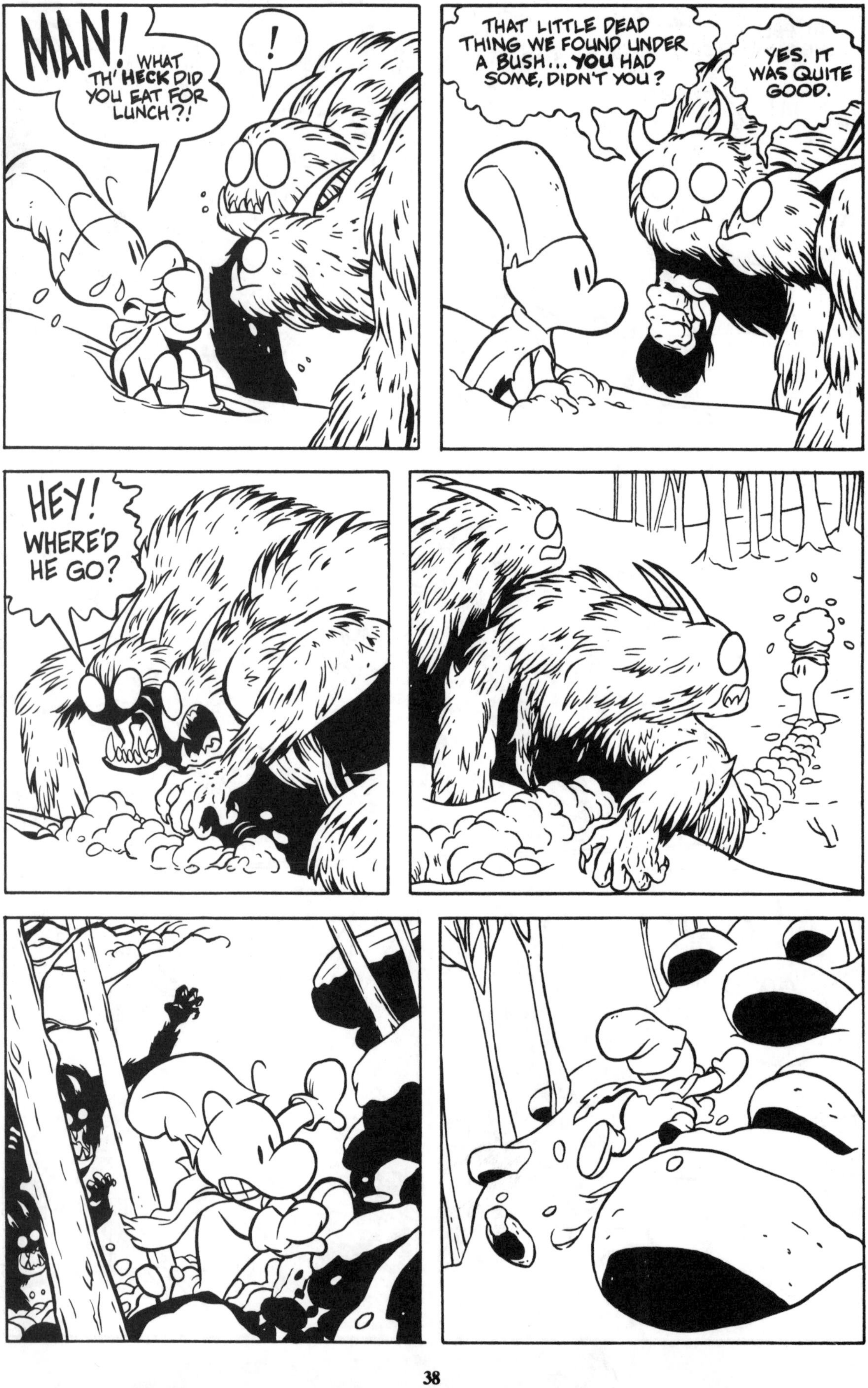
MAN! WHAT TH' HECK DID YOU EAT FOR LUNCH?!
!
THAT LITTLE DEAD THING WE FOUND UNDER A BUSH... YOU HAD SOME, DIDN'T YOU?
YES. IT WAS QUITE GOOD.
HEY! WHERE'D HE GO?

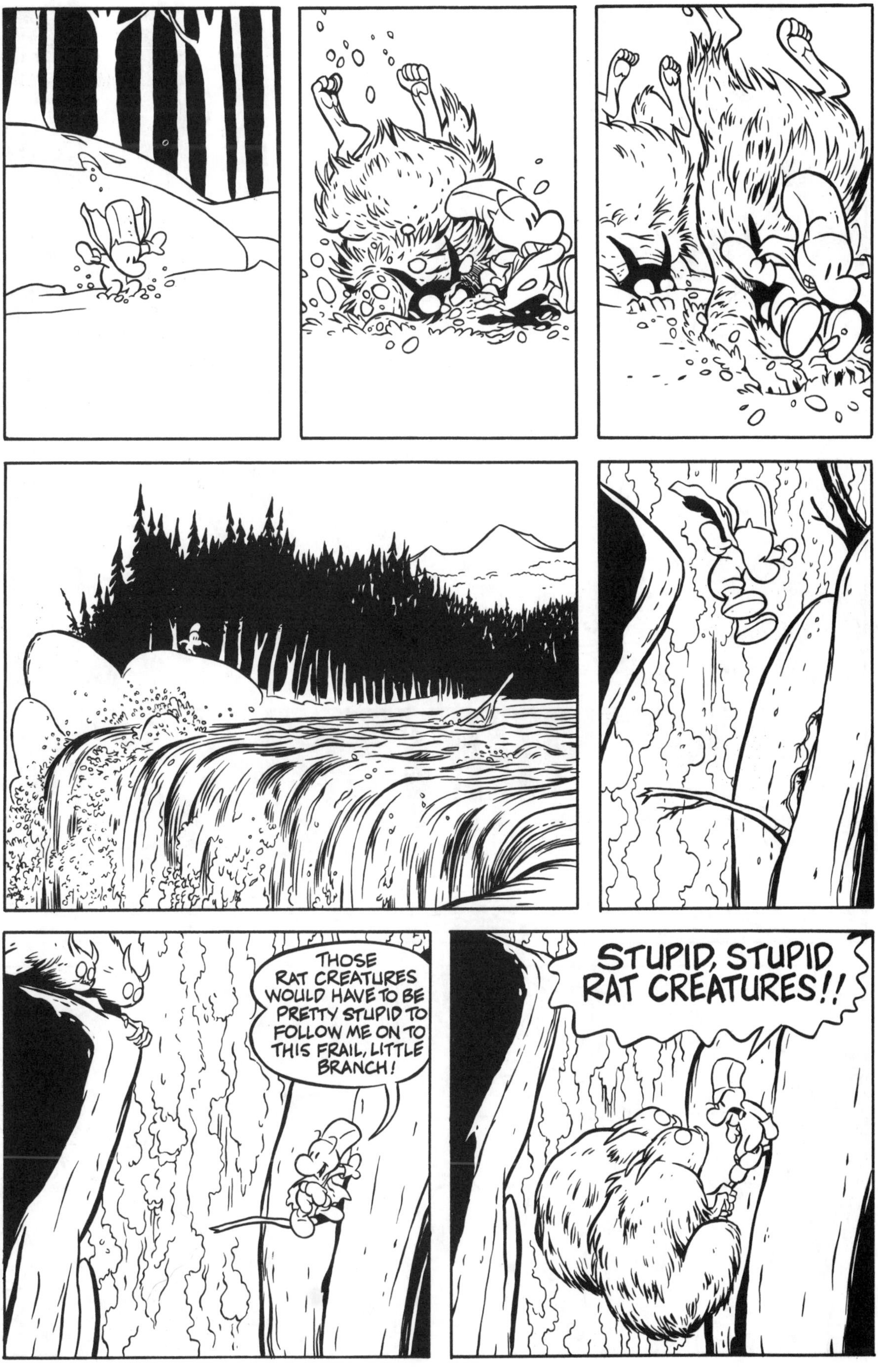
THOSE RAT CREATURES WOULD HAVE TO BE PRETTY STUPID TO FOLLOW ME ON TO THIS FRAIL, LITTLE BRANCH!
STUPID, STUPID RAT CREATURES!!

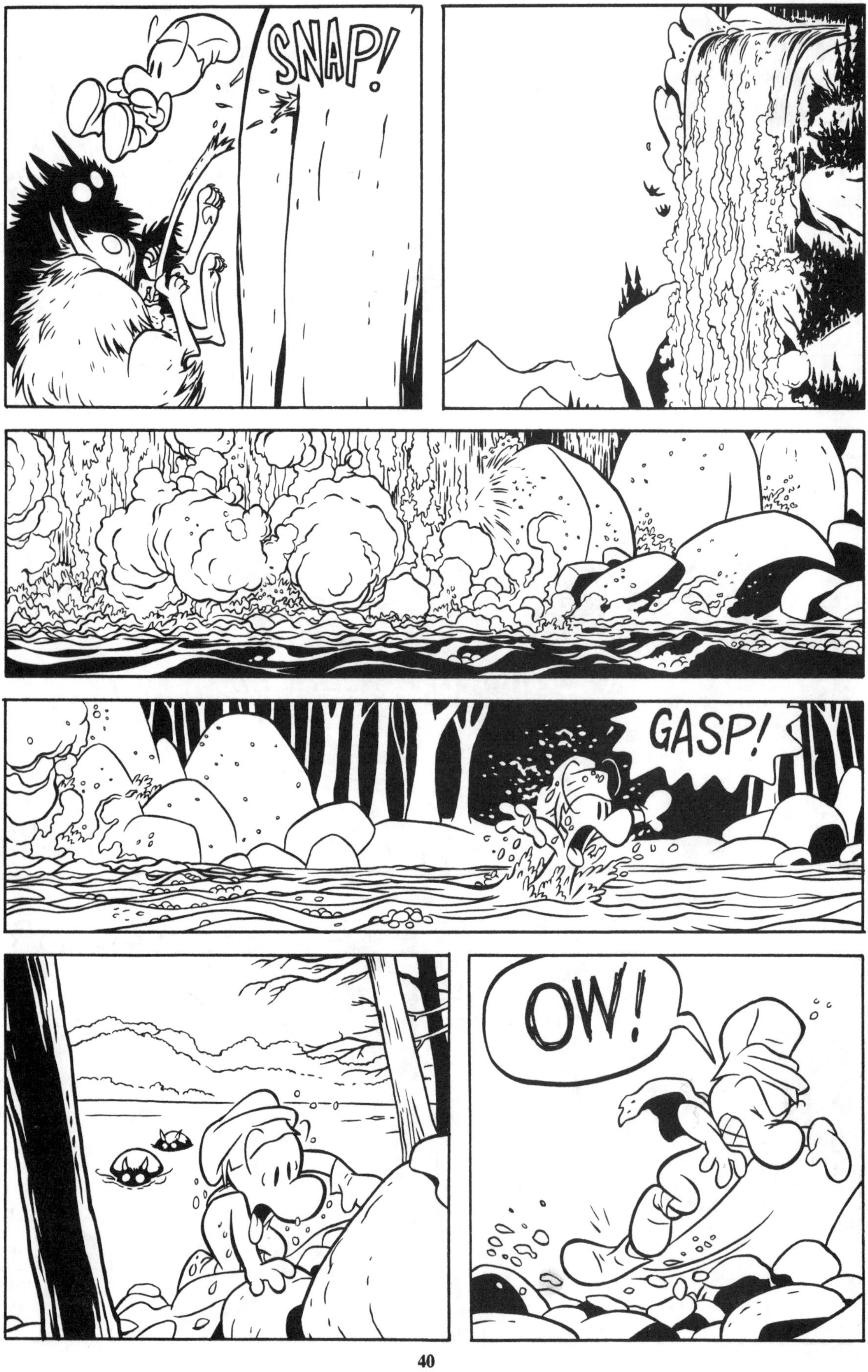
SNAP!
GASP!
OW!

42

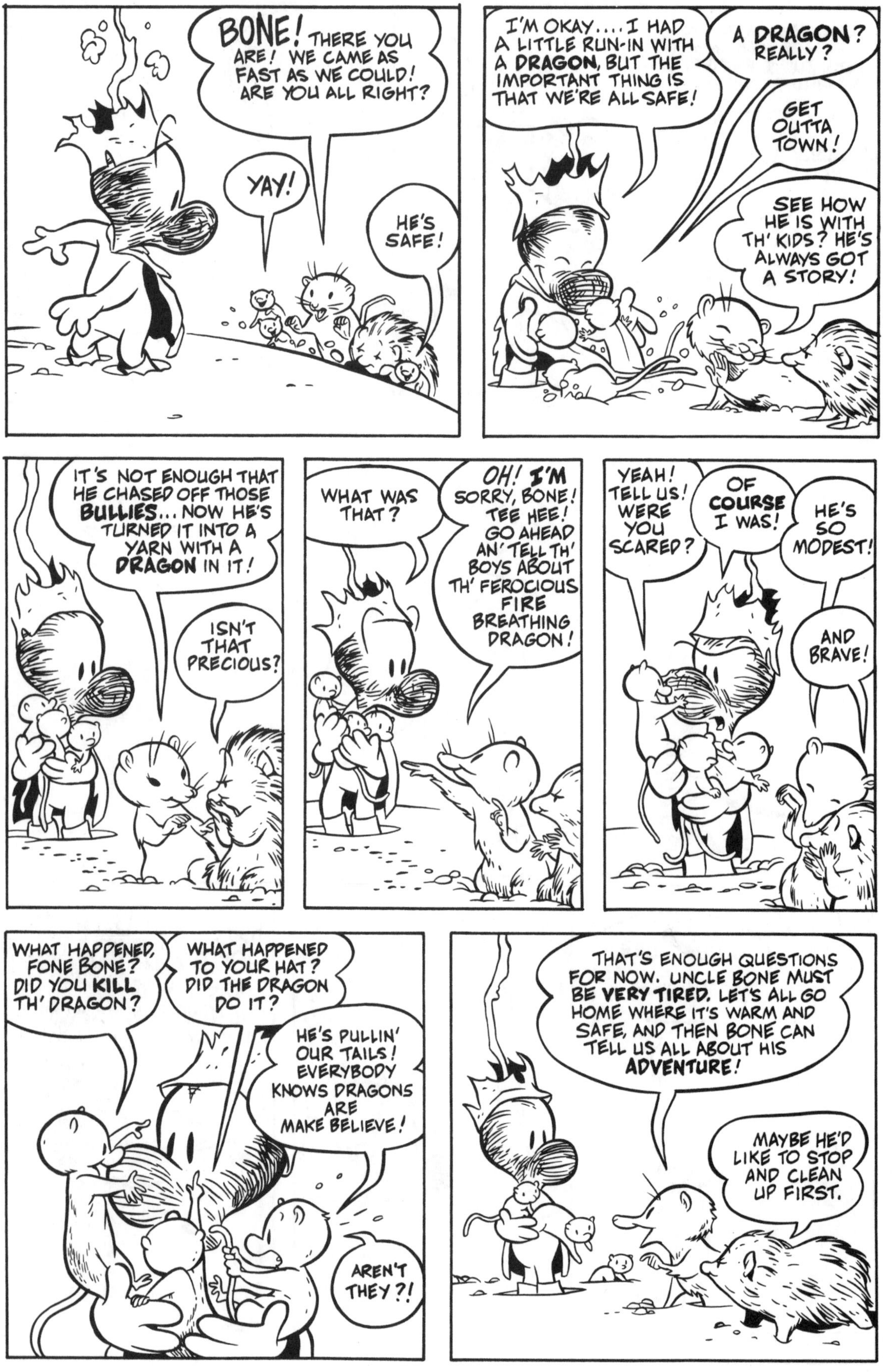
BONE! THERE YOU ARE! WE CAME AS FAST AS WE COULD! ARE YOU ALL RIGHT?
YAY!
HE'S SAFE!
I'M OKAY.... I HAD A LITTLE RUN-IN WITH A DRAGON, BUT THE IMPORTANT THING IS THAT WE'RE ALL SAFE!
A DRAGON? REALLY?
GET OUTTA TOWN!
SEE HOW HE IS WITH TH' KIDS? HE'S ALWAYS GOT A STORY!
IT'S NOT ENOUGH THAT HE CHASED OFF THOSE BULLIES... NOW HE'S TURNED IT INTO A YARN WITH A DRAGON IN IT!
ISN'T THAT PRECIOUS?
WHAT WAS THAT?
OH! I'M SORRY, BONE! TEE HEE! GO AHEAD AN' TELL TH' BOYS ABOUT TH' FEROCIOUS FIRE BREATHING DRAGON!
YEAH! TELL US! WERE YOU SCARED?
OF COURSE I WAS!
HE'S SO MODEST!
AND BRAVE!
WHAT HAPPENED, FONE BONE? DID YOU KILL TH' DRAGON?
WHAT HAPPENED TO YOUR HAT? DID THE DRAGON DO IT?
HE'S PULLIN' OUR TAILS! EVERYBODY KNOWS DRAGONS ARE MAKE BELIEVE!
AREN'T THEY?!
THAT'S ENOUGH QUESTIONS FOR NOW. UNCLE BONE MUST BE VERY TIRED. LET'S ALL GO HOME WHERE IT'S WARM AND SAFE, AND THEN BONE CAN TELL US ALL ABOUT HIS ADVENTURE!
MAYBE HE'D LIKE TO STOP AND CLEAN UP FIRST.

OH, YES! BY ALL **MEANS**! THERE'S A NICE, HOT **SPRING** JUST BACK OVER TH' HILL! WHY DON'T YOU STOP THERE TO FRESHEN UP! C'MON ALONG, BOYS! SAY THANK YOU TO UNCLE BONE!

THANK YOU!

DID HE REALLY SEE A DRAGON?

NOW DEAR...

HMMF! DID **TOO** SEE A DRAGON!

WHAT DO THEY **THINK**? I LIT MY HEAD ON FIRE TO KEEP WARM?

...AN' HOW COME THAT DRAGON KNEW I WAS BABYSITTING TH' **POSSUM** KIDS? WHAT'S HE DOIN'? **FOLLOWIN'** ME AROUND?

THIS PLACE IS **TOO** WIERD! THE FIRST SIGN OF SPRING I SEE.... **POW!** I'M TAKIN' OFF **RIGHT** THROUGH THOSE MOUNTAINS! WITH OR **WITHOUT** MY COUSINS!

SNAP!

UH, OH, WHAT WAS THAT?

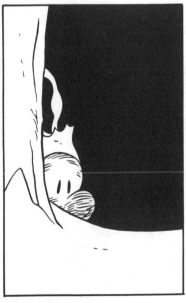

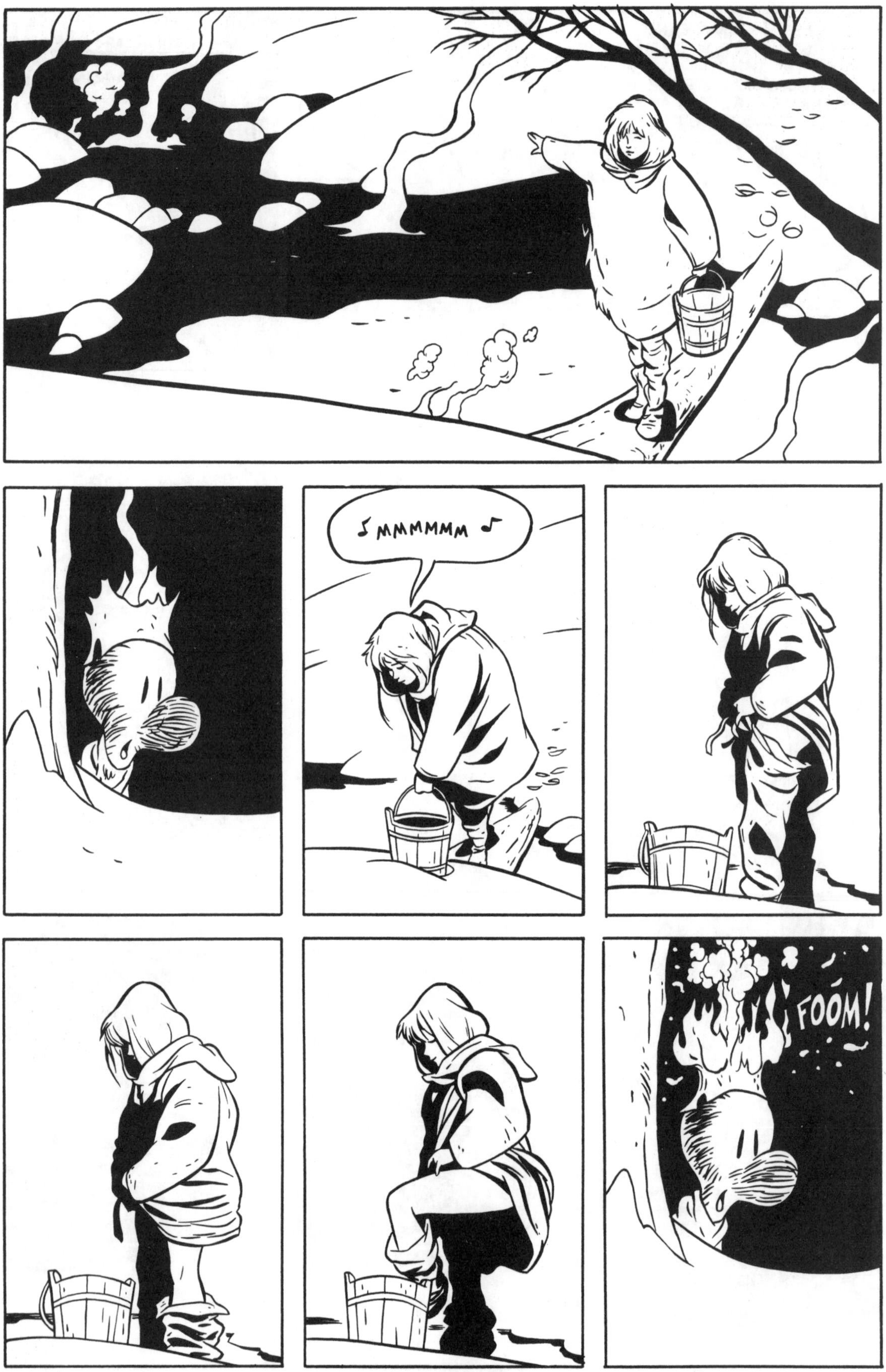
MMMMMM
FOOM!

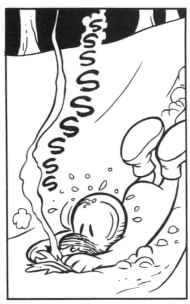

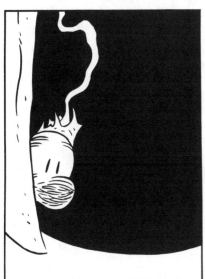

48

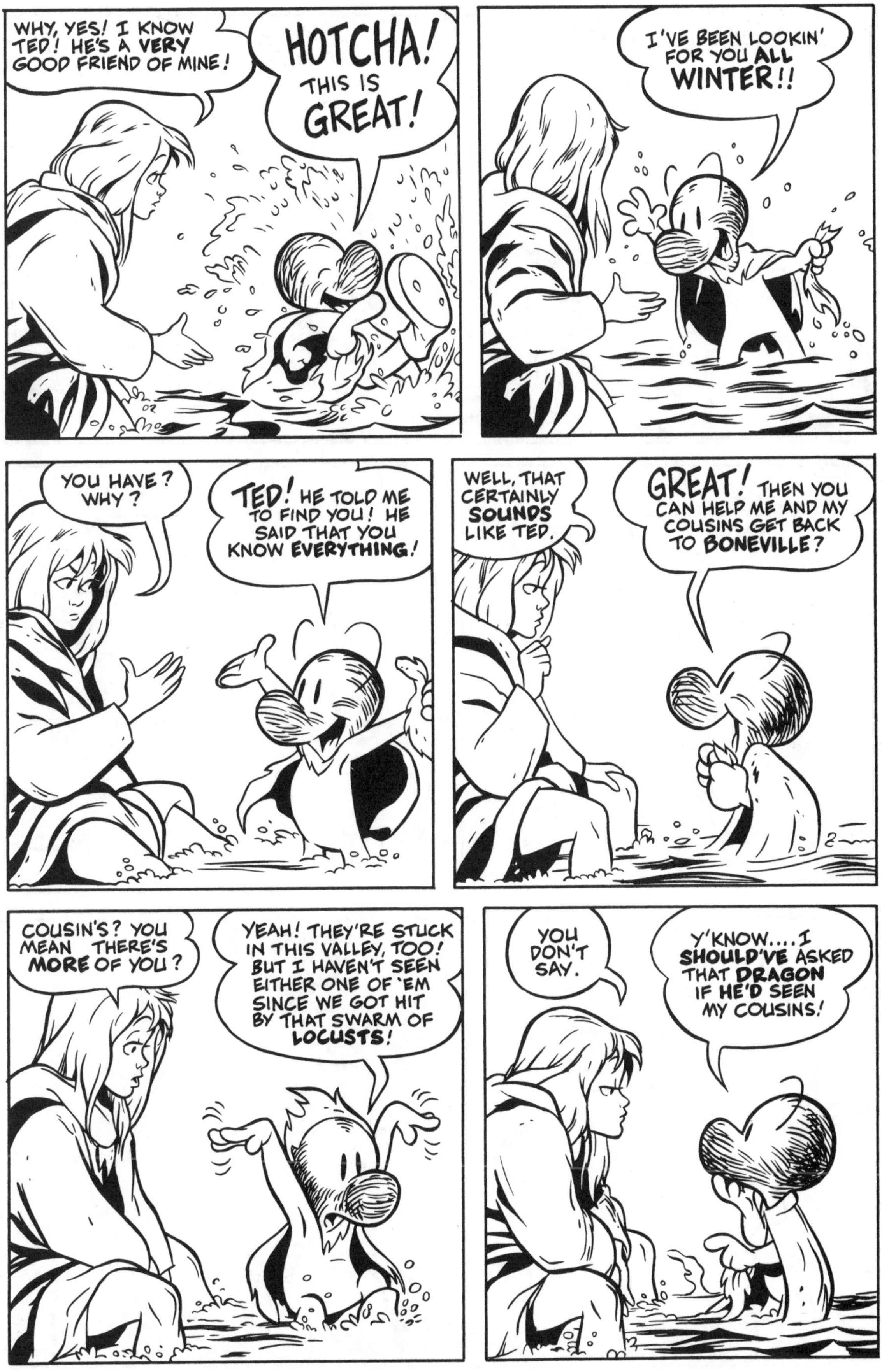
WHY, YES! I KNOW TED! HE'S A VERY GOOD FRIEND OF MINE!
HOTCHA! THIS IS GREAT!
I'VE BEEN LOOKIN' FOR YOU ALL WINTER!!
YOU HAVE? WHY?
TED! HE TOLD ME TO FIND YOU! HE SAID THAT YOU KNOW EVERYTHING!
WELL, THAT CERTAINLY SOUNDS LIKE TED.
GREAT! THEN YOU CAN HELP ME AND MY COUSINS GET BACK TO BONEVILLE?
COUSIN'S? YOU MEAN THERE'S MORE OF YOU?
YEAH! THEY'RE STUCK IN THIS VALLEY, TOO! BUT I HAVEN'T SEEN EITHER ONE OF 'EM SINCE WE GOT HIT BY THAT SWARM OF LOCUSTS!
YOU DON'T SAY.
Y'KNOW.... I SHOULD'VE ASKED THAT DRAGON IF HE'D SEEN MY COUSINS!

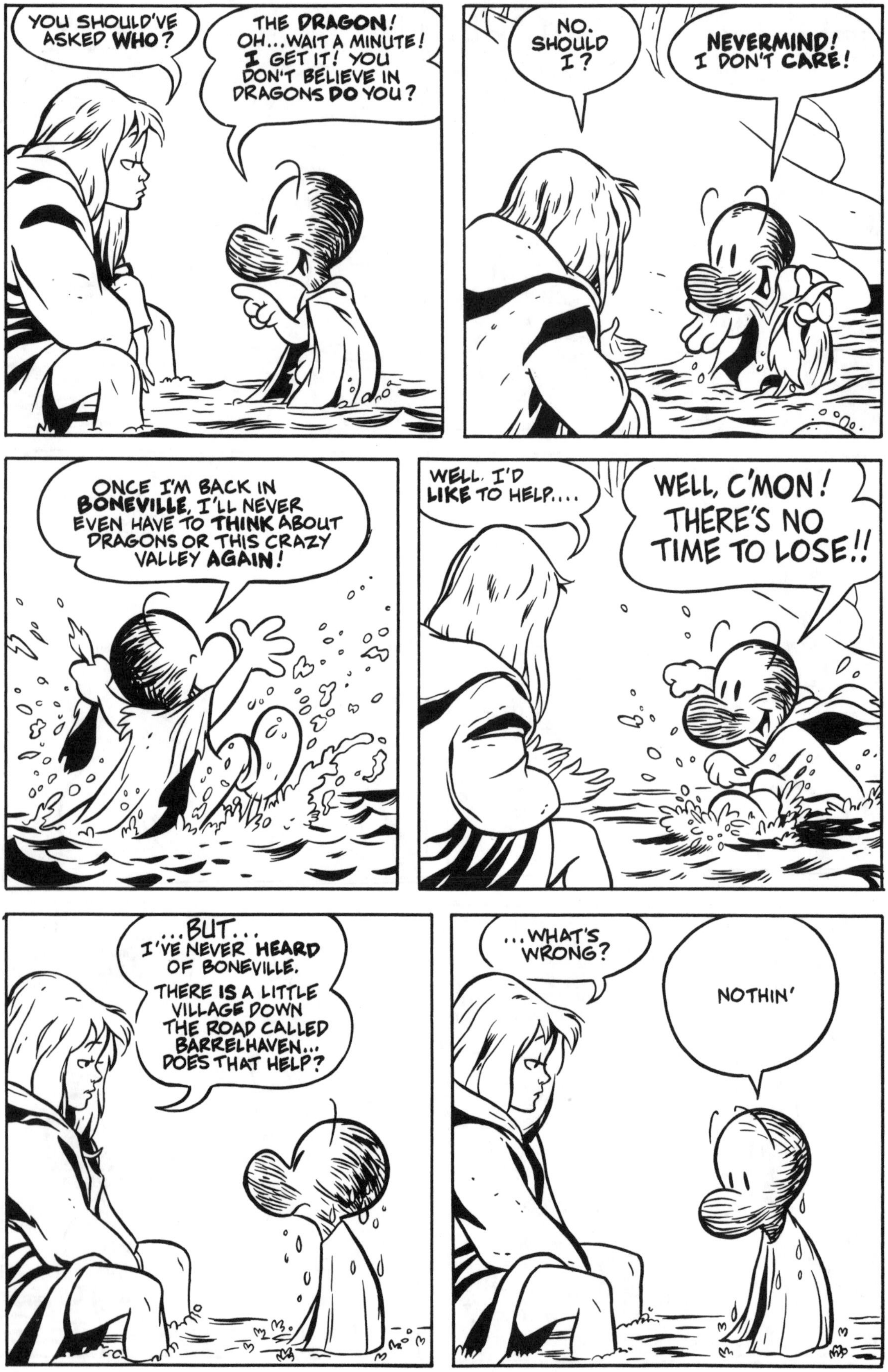
YOU SHOULD'VE ASKED WHO?
THE DRAGON! OH... WAIT A MINUTE! I GET IT! YOU DON'T BELIEVE IN DRAGONS DO YOU?
NO. SHOULD I?
NEVERMIND! I DON'T CARE!
ONCE I'M BACK IN BONEVILLE, I'LL NEVER EVEN HAVE TO THINK ABOUT DRAGONS OR THIS CRAZY VALLEY AGAIN!
WELL, I'D LIKE TO HELP....
WELL, C'MON! THERE'S NO TIME TO LOSE!!
...BUT... I'VE NEVER HEARD OF BONEVILLE.
THERE IS A LITTLE VILLAGE DOWN THE ROAD CALLED BARRELHAVEN... DOES THAT HELP?
...WHAT'S WRONG?
NOTHIN'

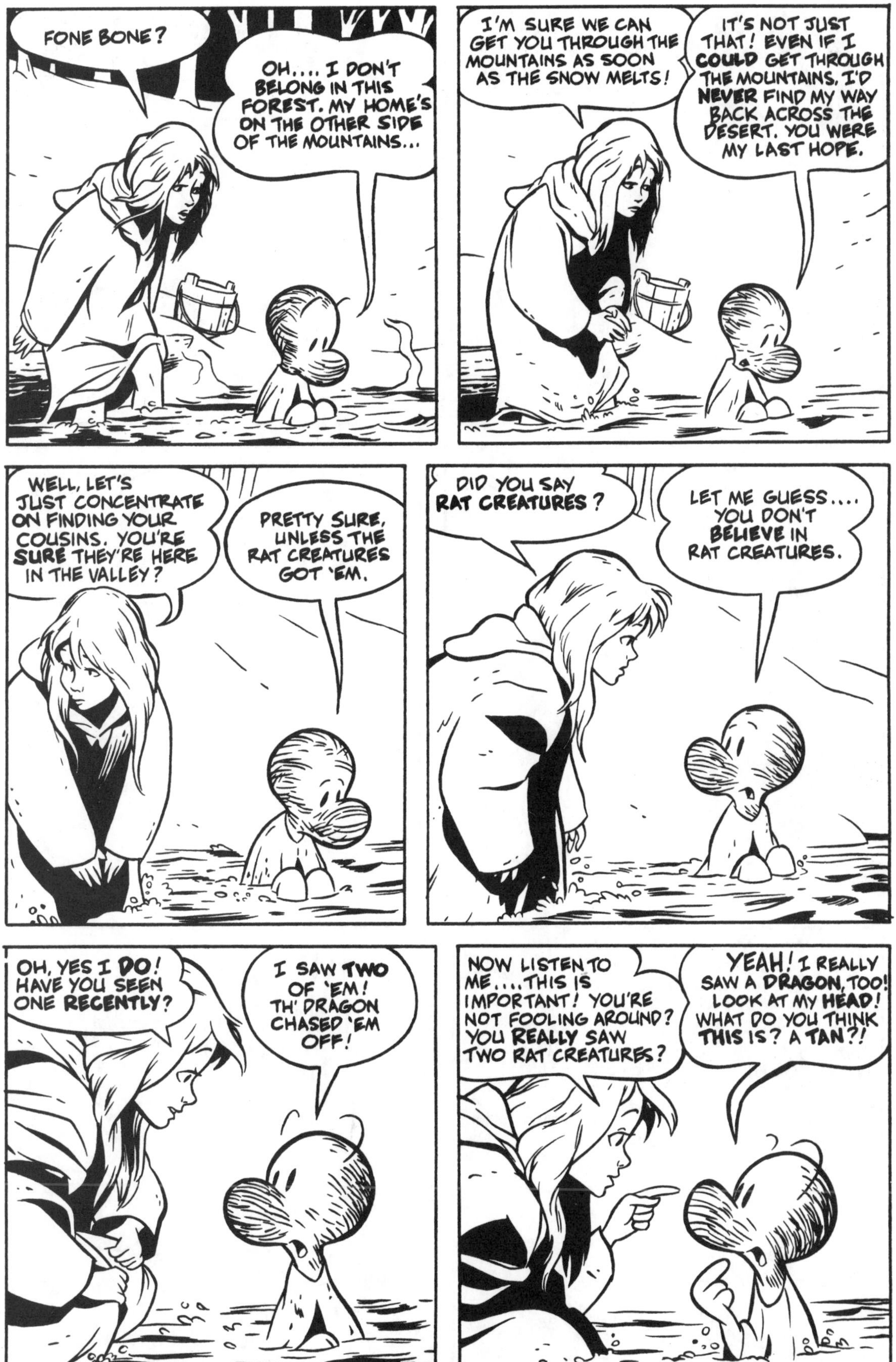
FONE BONE?
OH.... I DON'T BELONG IN THIS FOREST. MY HOME'S ON THE OTHER SIDE OF THE MOUNTAINS...
I'M SURE WE CAN GET YOU THROUGH THE MOUNTAINS AS SOON AS THE SNOW MELTS!
IT'S NOT JUST THAT! EVEN IF I COULD GET THROUGH THE MOUNTAINS, I'D NEVER FIND MY WAY BACK ACROSS THE DESERT. YOU WERE MY LAST HOPE.
WELL, LET'S JUST CONCENTRATE ON FINDING YOUR COUSINS. YOU'RE SURE THEY'RE HERE IN THE VALLEY?
PRETTY SURE, UNLESS THE RAT CREATURES GOT 'EM.
DID YOU SAY RAT CREATURES?
LET ME GUESS.... YOU DON'T BELIEVE IN RAT CREATURES.
OH, YES I DO! HAVE YOU SEEN ONE RECENTLY?
I SAW TWO OF 'EM! TH' DRAGON CHASED 'EM OFF!
NOW LISTEN TO ME....THIS IS IMPORTANT! YOU'RE NOT FOOLING AROUND? YOU REALLY SAW TWO RAT CREATURES?
YEAH! I REALLY SAW A DRAGON, TOO! LOOK AT MY HEAD! WHAT DO YOU THINK THIS IS? A TAN?!

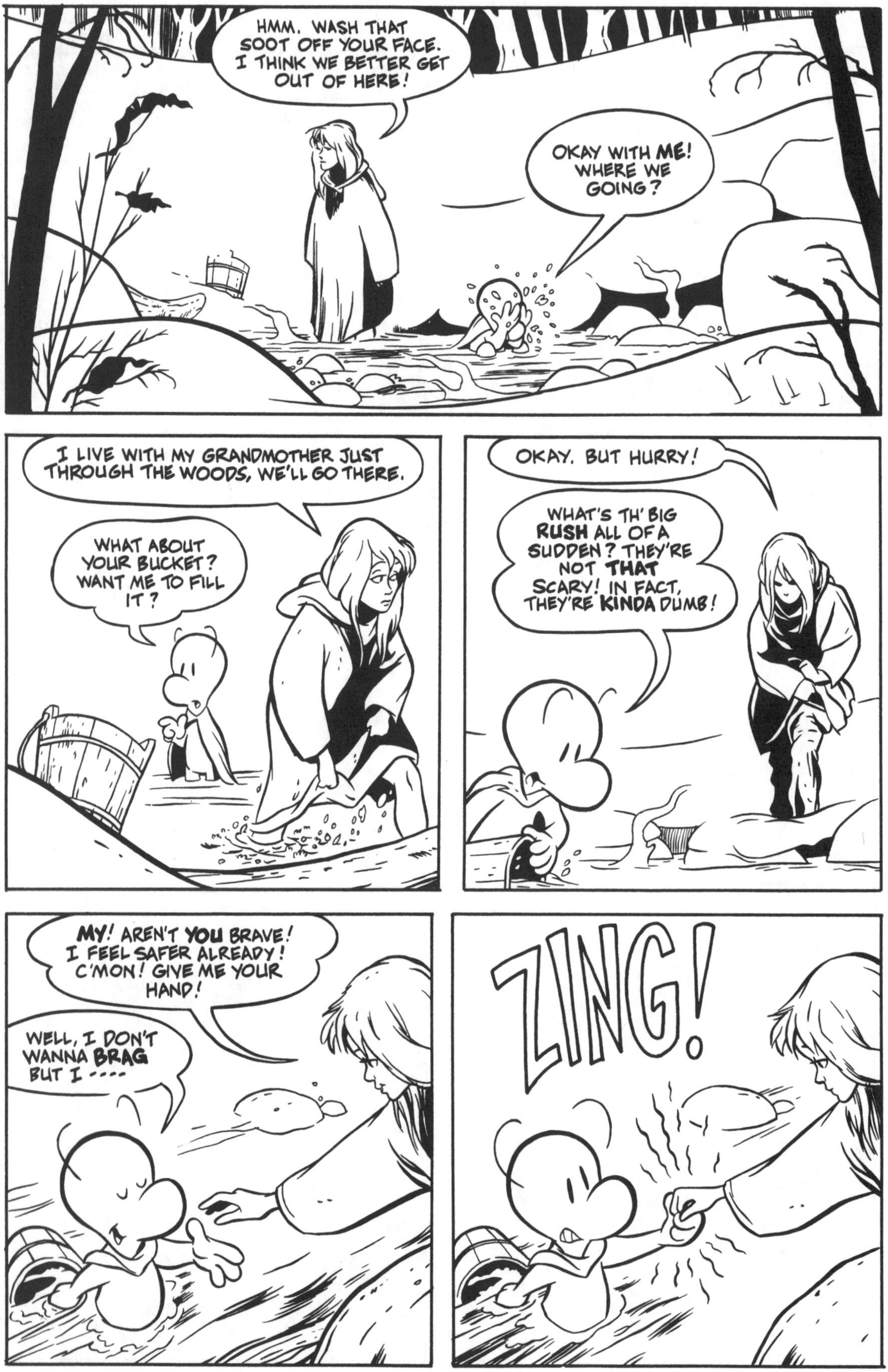
HMM. WASH THAT SOOT OFF YOUR FACE. I THINK WE BETTER GET OUT OF HERE!
OKAY WITH ME! WHERE WE GOING?
I LIVE WITH MY GRANDMOTHER JUST THROUGH THE WOODS, WE'LL GO THERE.
WHAT ABOUT YOUR BUCKET? WANT ME TO FILL IT?
OKAY. BUT HURRY!
WHAT'S TH' BIG RUSH ALL OF A SUDDEN? THEY'RE NOT THAT SCARY! IN FACT, THEY'RE KINDA DUMB!
MY! AREN'T YOU BRAVE! I FEEL SAFER ALREADY! C'MON! GIVE ME YOUR HAND!
WELL, I DON'T WANNA BRAG BUT I - - - -
ZING!

Next: Phoney Bone

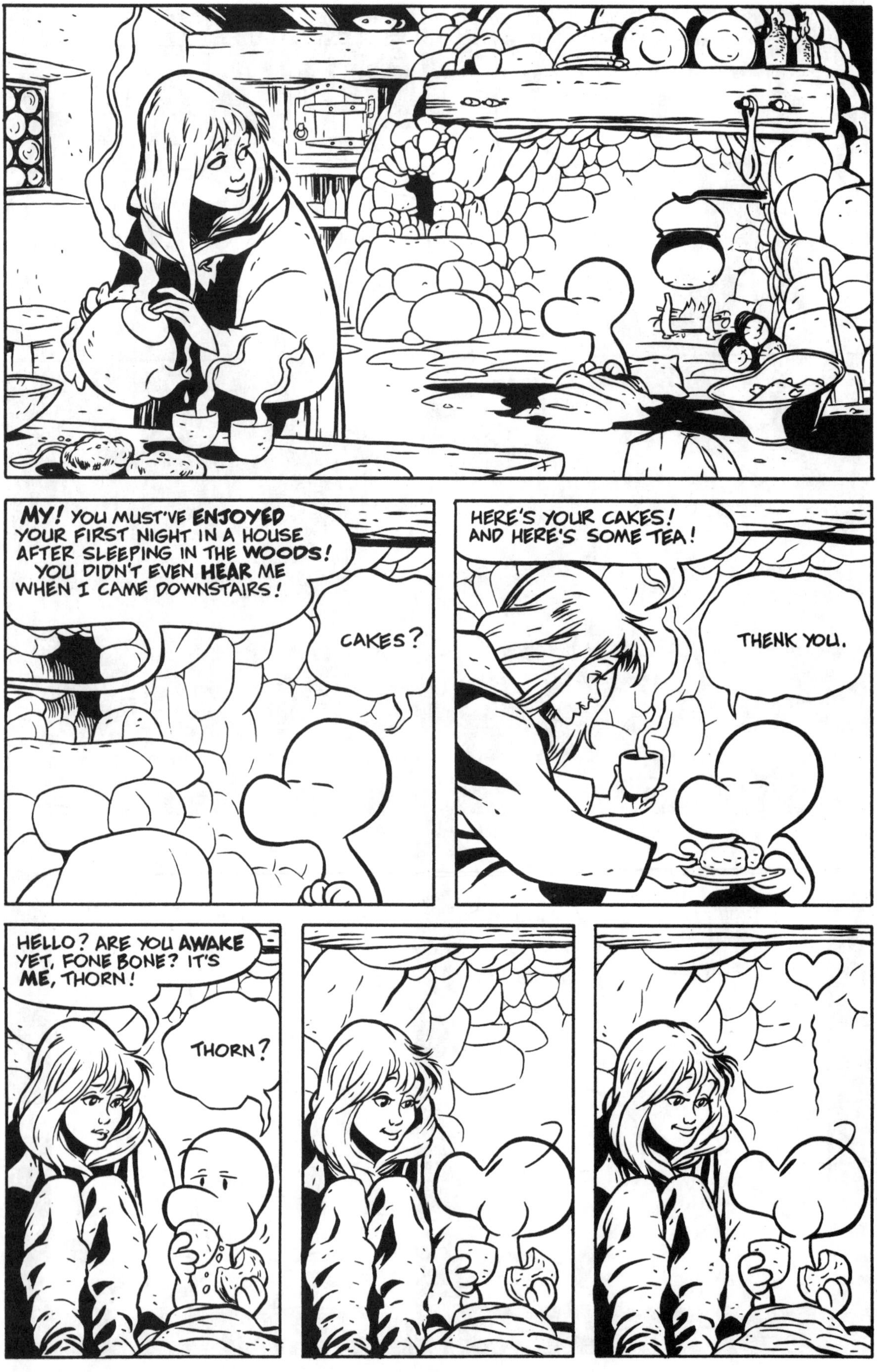
MY! YOU MUST'VE ENJOYED YOUR FIRST NIGHT IN A HOUSE AFTER SLEEPING IN THE WOODS! YOU DIDN'T EVEN HEAR ME WHEN I CAME DOWNSTAIRS!
CAKES?
HERE'S YOUR CAKES! AND HERE'S SOME TEA!
THENK YOU.
HELLO? ARE YOU AWAKE YET, FONE BONE? IT'S ME, THORN!
THORN?

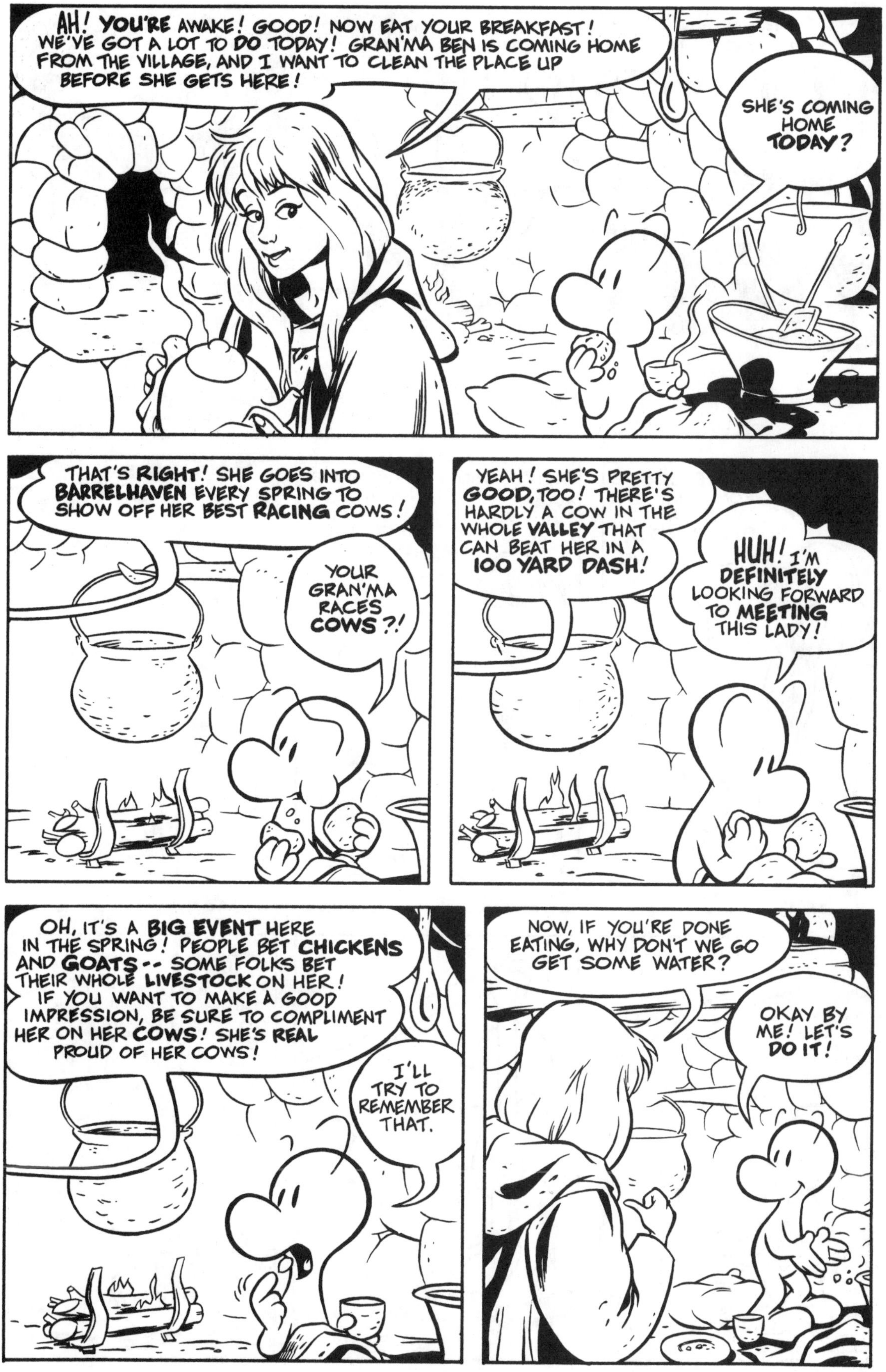
AH! YOU'RE AWAKE! GOOD! NOW EAT YOUR BREAKFAST! WE'VE GOT A LOT TO DO TODAY! GRAN'MA BEN IS COMING HOME FROM THE VILLAGE, AND I WANT TO CLEAN THE PLACE UP BEFORE SHE GETS HERE!
SHE'S COMING HOME TODAY?
THAT'S RIGHT! SHE GOES INTO BARRELHAVEN EVERY SPRING TO SHOW OFF HER BEST RACING COWS!
YOUR GRAN'MA RACES COWS?!
YEAH! SHE'S PRETTY GOOD, TOO! THERE'S HARDLY A COW IN THE WHOLE VALLEY THAT CAN BEAT HER IN A 100 YARD DASH!
HUH! I'M DEFINITELY LOOKING FORWARD TO MEETING THIS LADY!
OH, IT'S A BIG EVENT HERE IN THE SPRING! PEOPLE BET CHICKENS AND GOATS -- SOME FOLKS BET THEIR WHOLE LIVESTOCK ON HER! IF YOU WANT TO MAKE A GOOD IMPRESSION, BE SURE TO COMPLIMENT HER ON HER COWS! SHE'S REAL PROUD OF HER COWS!
I'LL TRY TO REMEMBER THAT.
NOW, IF YOU'RE DONE EATING, WHY DON'T WE GO GET SOME WATER?
OKAY BY ME! LET'S DO IT!

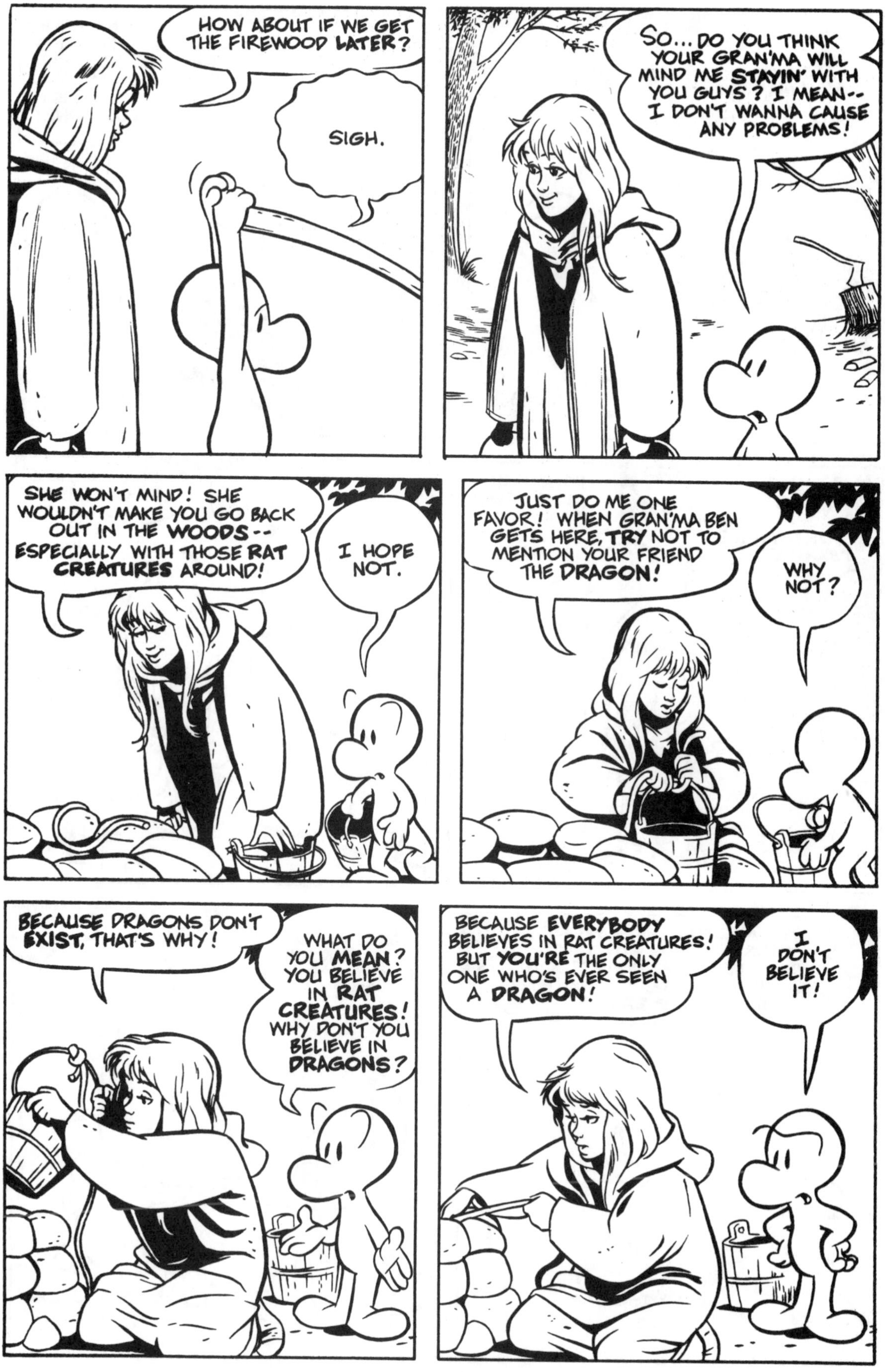
HOW ABOUT IF WE GET THE FIREWOOD LATER?
SIGH.
SO... DO YOU THINK YOUR GRAN'MA WILL MIND ME STAYIN' WITH YOU GUYS? I MEAN-- I DON'T WANNA CAUSE ANY PROBLEMS!
SHE WON'T MIND! SHE WOULDN'T MAKE YOU GO BACK OUT IN THE WOODS-- ESPECIALLY WITH THOSE RAT CREATURES AROUND!
I HOPE NOT.
JUST DO ME ONE FAVOR! WHEN GRAN'MA BEN GETS HERE, TRY NOT TO MENTION YOUR FRIEND THE DRAGON!
WHY NOT?
BECAUSE DRAGONS DON'T EXIST, THAT'S WHY!
WHAT DO YOU MEAN? YOU BELIEVE IN RAT CREATURES! WHY DON'T YOU BELIEVE IN DRAGONS?
BECAUSE EVERYBODY BELIEVES IN RAT CREATURES! BUT YOU'RE THE ONLY ONE WHO'S EVER SEEN A DRAGON!
I DON'T BELIEVE IT!

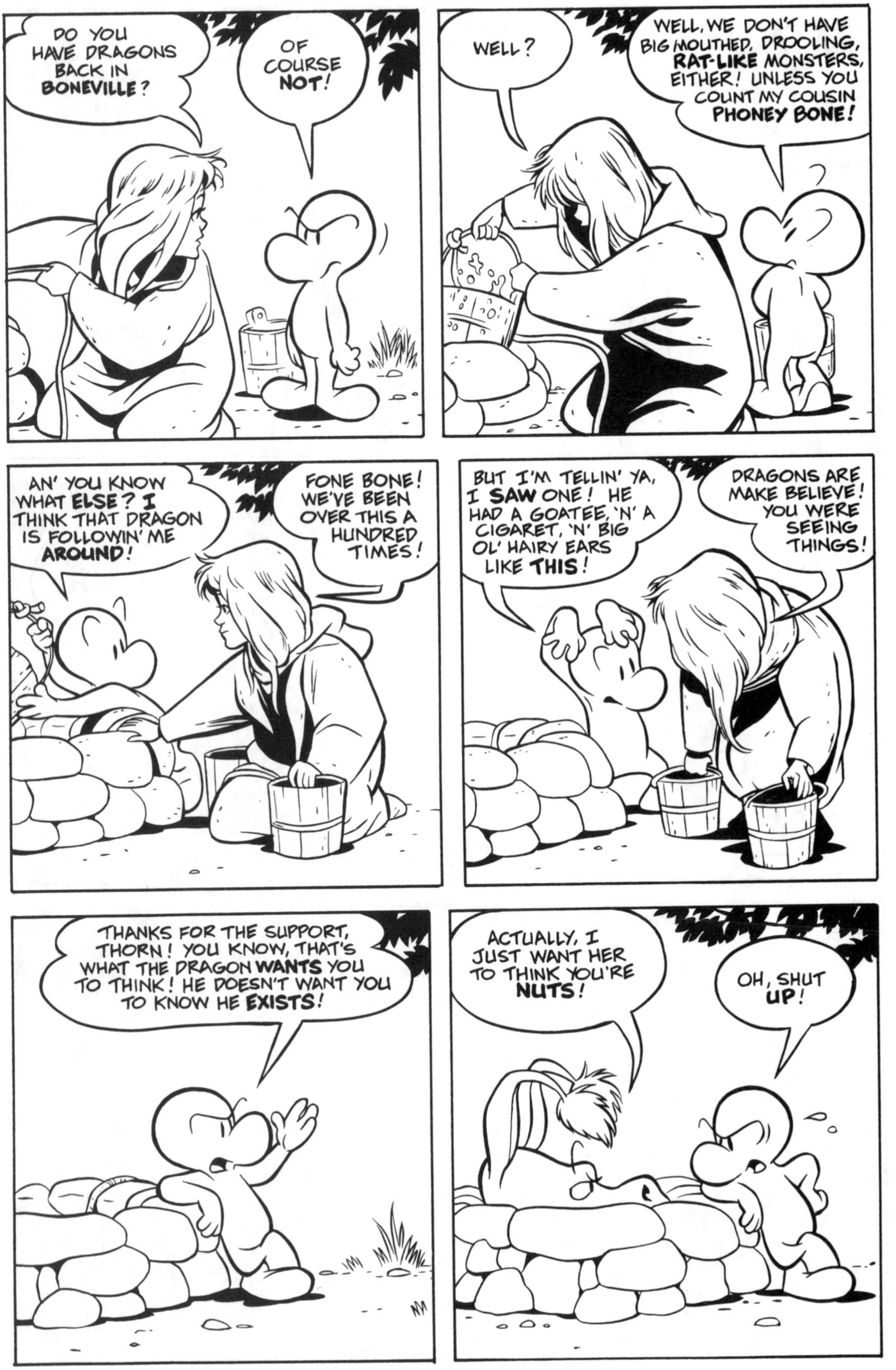

DO YOU HAVE DRAGONS BACK IN BONEVILLE?
OF COURSE NOT!
WELL?
WELL, WE DON'T HAVE BIG MOUTHED, DROOLING, RAT-LIKE MONSTERS, EITHER! UNLESS YOU COUNT MY COUSIN PHONEY BONE!
AN' YOU KNOW WHAT ELSE? I THINK THAT DRAGON IS FOLLOWIN' ME AROUND!
FONE BONE! WE'VE BEEN OVER THIS A HUNDRED TIMES!
BUT I'M TELLIN' YA, I SAW ONE! HE HAD A GOATEE, 'N' A CIGARET, 'N' BIG OL' HAIRY EARS LIKE THIS!
DRAGONS ARE MAKE BELIEVE! YOU WERE SEEING THINGS!
THANKS FOR THE SUPPORT, THORN! YOU KNOW, THAT'S WHAT THE DRAGON WANTS YOU TO THINK! HE DOESN'T WANT YOU TO KNOW HE EXISTS!
ACTUALLY, I JUST WANT HER TO THINK YOU'RE NUTS!
OH, SHUT UP!

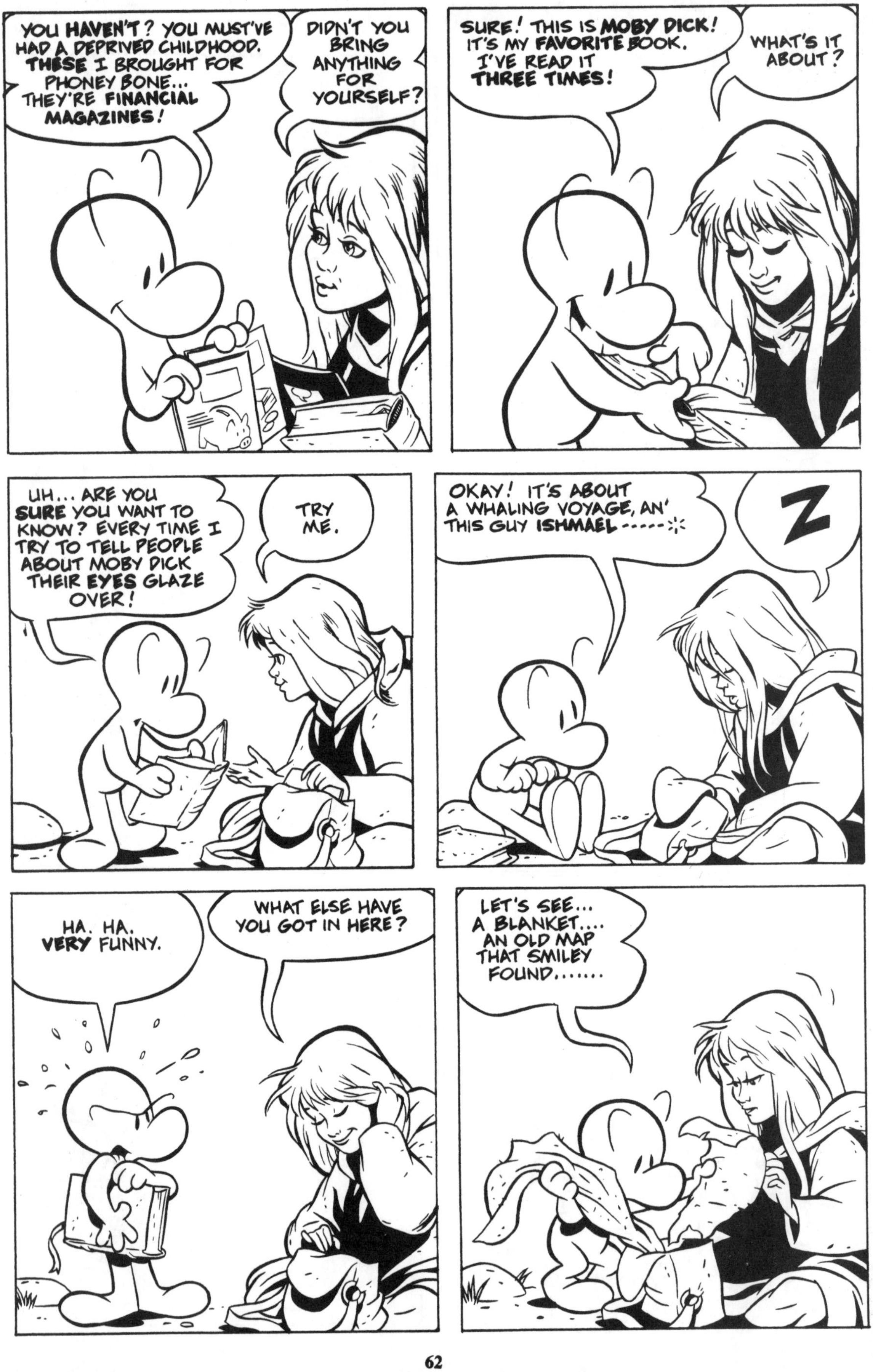
YOU HAVEN'T? YOU MUST'VE HAD A DEPRIVED CHILDHOOD. THESE I BROUGHT FOR PHONEY BONE... THEY'RE FINANCIAL MAGAZINES!
DIDN'T YOU BRING ANYTHING FOR YOURSELF?
SURE! THIS IS MOBY DICK! IT'S MY FAVORITE BOOK. I'VE READ IT THREE TIMES!
WHAT'S IT ABOUT?
UH... ARE YOU SURE YOU WANT TO KNOW? EVERY TIME I TRY TO TELL PEOPLE ABOUT MOBY DICK THEIR EYES GLAZE OVER!
TRY ME.
OKAY! IT'S ABOUT A WHALING VOYAGE, AN' THIS GUY ISHMAEL-----
Z
HA. HA. VERY FUNNY.
WHAT ELSE HAVE YOU GOT IN HERE?
LET'S SEE... A BLANKET.... AN OLD MAP THAT SMILEY FOUND.......

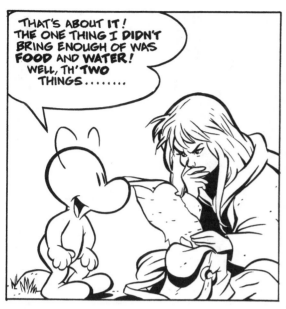

THAT'S ABOUT IT! THE ONE THING I DIDN'T BRING ENOUGH OF WAS **FOOD** AND **WATER**! WELL, TH' **TWO** THINGS........

WHY ARE YOU MAKING THAT FACE?

I DON'T KNOW.... SOMETHING ABOUT THIS MAP IS FAMILIAR...

REALLY? SMILEY FOUND IT OUT IN TH' DESERT RIGHT BEFORE WE GOT SPLIT UP.

IT REMINDS ME OF A DREAM I USED TO HAVE...

WHOA. AND YOU THINK **MY** STORIES ARE STRANGE!

ARE YOU OKAY?

I'M FINE. LET'S JUST FORGET IT. C'MON. GRAN'MA WILL BE HERE SOON....

GRUMP! GRUMP! GRUMP!

GRUMP!

SPLOP

SPLOOSH

OOOH! WAIT'LL I GET MY HANDS ON THAT COUSIN OF MINE!

I CAN'T **BELIEVE** FONE BONE WOULD JUST **LEAVE** ME OUT HERE WANDERING AROUND HELPLESS AND HUNGRY!

I'LL BET HE'S BACK IN BONEVILLE **RIGHT NOW**, SITTING IN **MY** HOUSE, EATING **MY** FOOD!

GLORP!

RUMBLE!

GRRRR

GROWL!

HEY! **SHUT UP!** I JUST ATE A **STICK** AN HOUR AGO! WHAT DO YOU **WANT** FROM ME?!

64

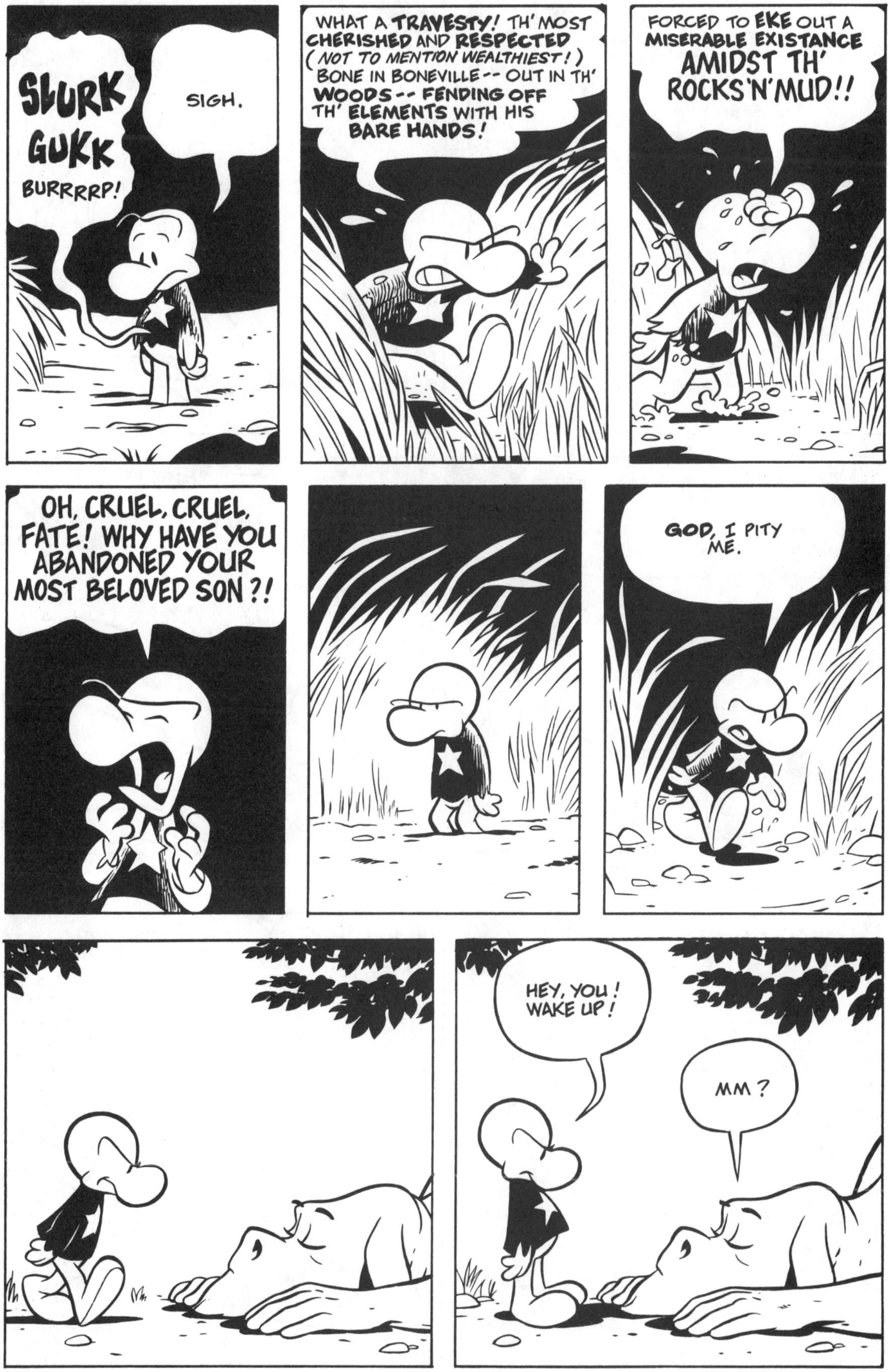
SLURK
GUKK
BURRRRP!
SIGH.
WHAT A TRAVESTY! TH' MOST CHERISHED AND RESPECTED (NOT TO MENTION WEALTHIEST!) BONE IN BONEVILLE -- OUT IN TH' WOODS -- FENDING OFF TH' ELEMENTS WITH HIS BARE HANDS!
FORCED TO EKE OUT A MISERABLE EXISTANCE AMIDST TH' ROCKS 'N' MUD!!
OH, CRUEL, CRUEL, FATE! WHY HAVE YOU ABANDONED YOUR MOST BELOVED SON?!
GOD, I PITY ME.
HEY, YOU! WAKE UP!
MM?

66

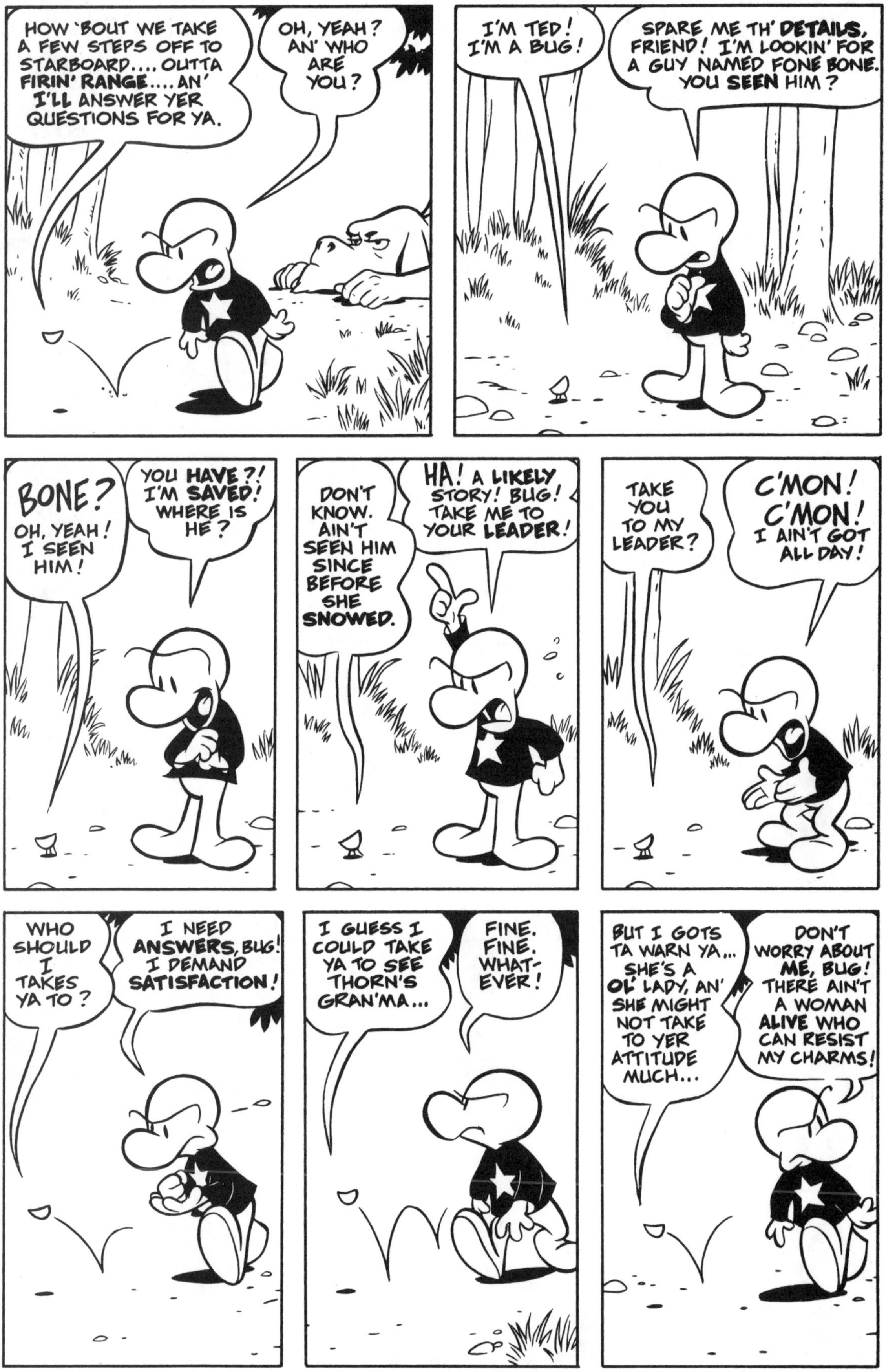
HOW 'BOUT WE TAKE A FEW STEPS OFF TO STARBOARD.... OUTTA FIRIN' RANGE.... AN' I'LL ANSWER YER QUESTIONS FOR YA.
OH, YEAH? AN' WHO ARE YOU?
I'M TED! I'M A BUG!
SPARE ME TH' DETAILS, FRIEND! I'M LOOKIN' FOR A GUY NAMED FONE BONE. YOU SEEN HIM?
BONE? OH, YEAH! I SEEN HIM!
YOU HAVE?! I'M SAVED! WHERE IS HE?
DON'T KNOW. AIN'T SEEN HIM SINCE BEFORE SHE SNOWED.
HA! A LIKELY STORY! BUG! TAKE ME TO YOUR LEADER!
TAKE YOU TO MY LEADER?
C'MON! C'MON! I AIN'T GOT ALL DAY!
WHO SHOULD I TAKES YA TO?
I NEED ANSWERS, BUG! I DEMAND SATISFACTION!
I GUESS I COULD TAKE YA TO SEE THORN'S GRAN'MA...
FINE. FINE. WHAT-EVER!
BUT I GOTS TA WARN YA... SHE'S A OL' LADY, AN' SHE MIGHT NOT TAKE TO YER ATTITUDE MUCH...
DON'T WORRY ABOUT ME, BUG! THERE AIN'T A WOMAN ALIVE WHO CAN RESIST MY CHARMS!

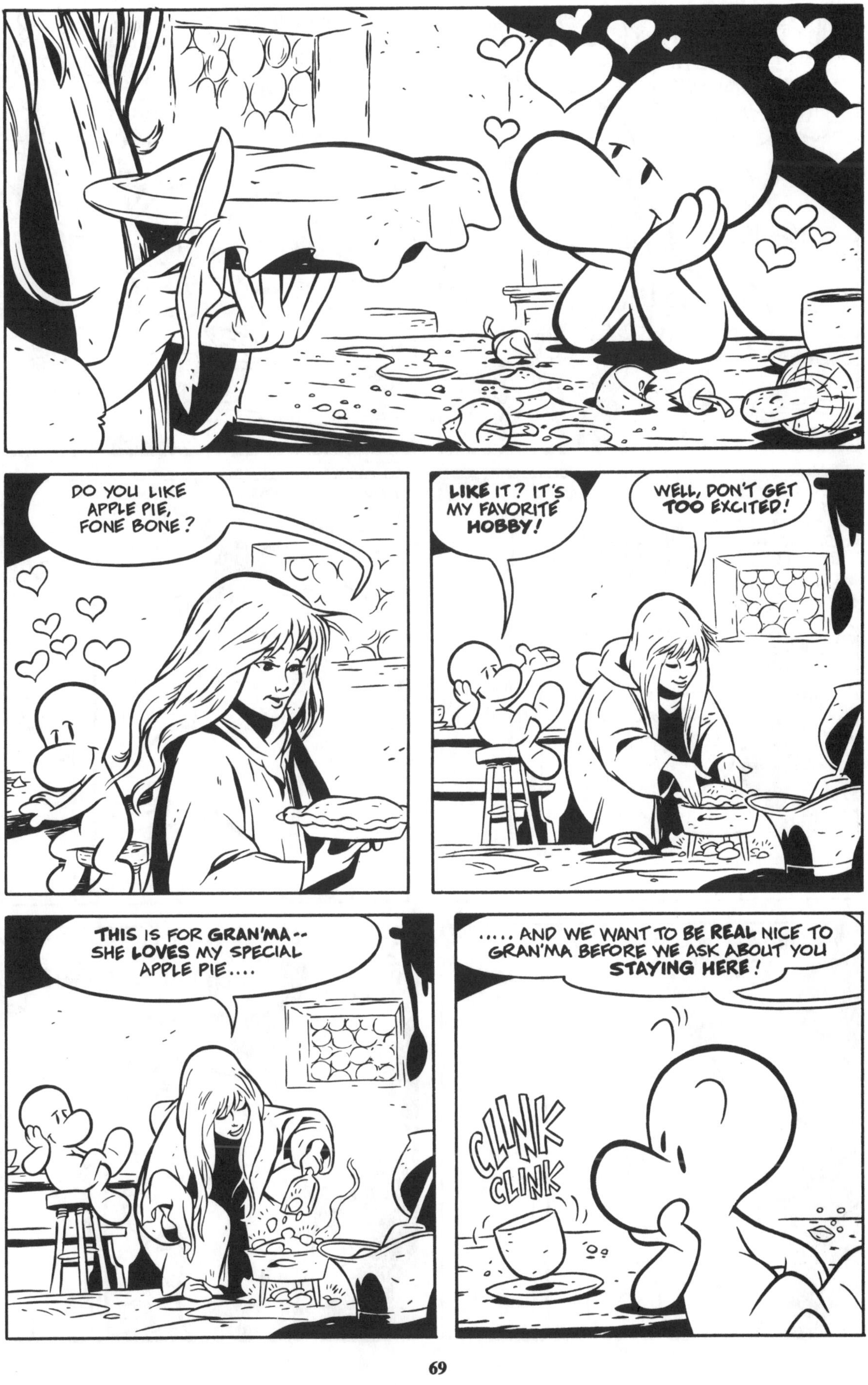
DO YOU LIKE APPLE PIE, FONE BONE?
LIKE IT? IT'S MY FAVORITE HOBBY!
WELL, DON'T GET TOO EXCITED!
THIS IS FOR GRAN'MA-- SHE LOVES MY SPECIAL APPLE PIE....
..... AND WE WANT TO BE REAL NICE TO GRAN'MA BEFORE WE ASK ABOUT YOU STAYING HERE!
CLINK
CLINK

70

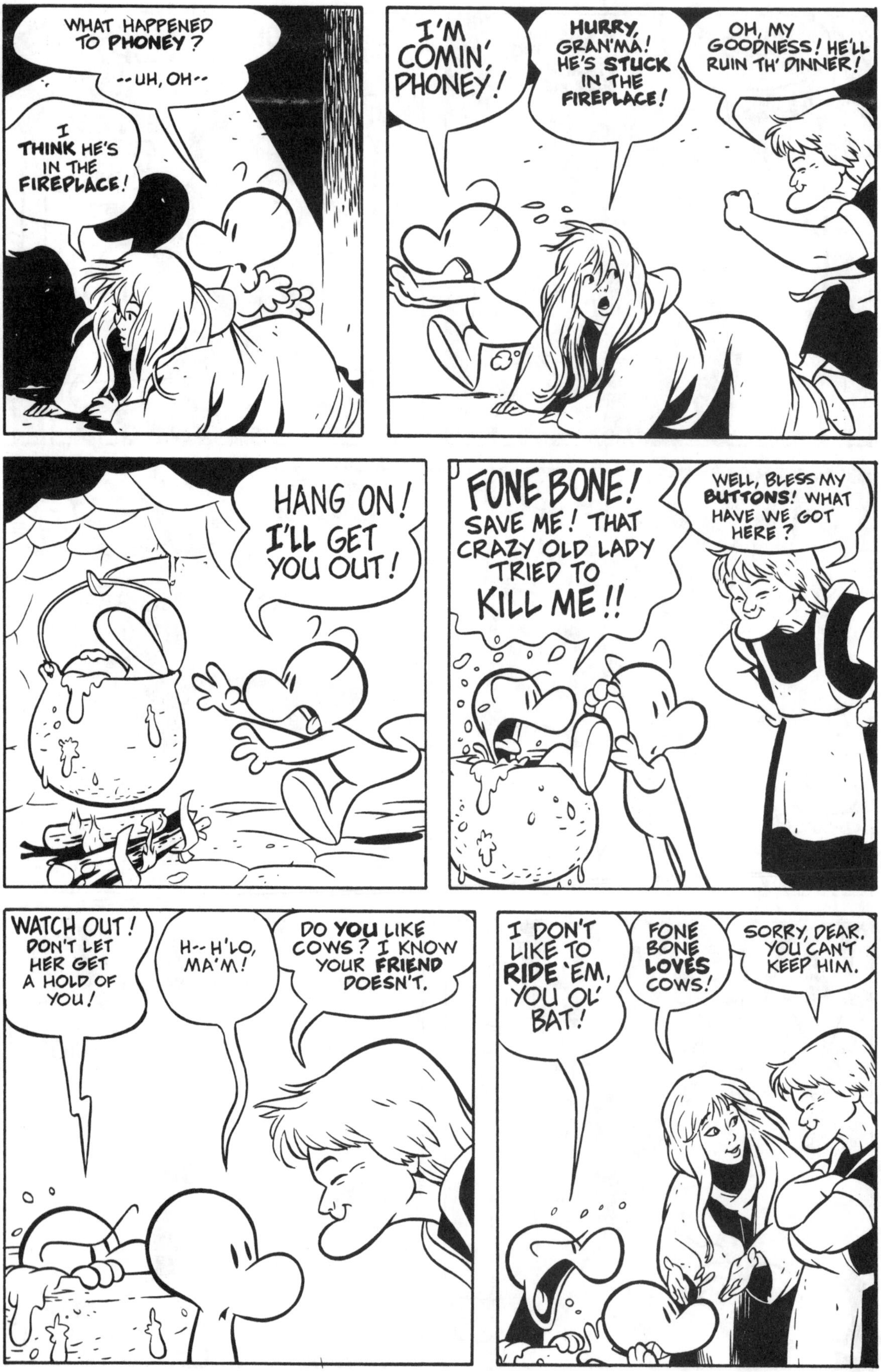
WHAT HAPPENED TO **PHONEY** ?
--UH, OH--
I **THINK** HE'S IN THE **FIREPLACE**!
I'M COMIN', PHONEY!
HURRY, GRAN'MA! HE'S **STUCK** IN THE **FIREPLACE**!
OH, MY GOODNESS! HE'LL RUIN TH' DINNER!
HANG ON! **I'LL** GET YOU OUT!
FONE BONE! SAVE ME! THAT CRAZY OLD LADY TRIED TO KILL ME!!
WELL, BLESS MY **BUTTONS**! WHAT HAVE WE GOT HERE?
WATCH OUT! **DON'T LET HER GET** A HOLD OF YOU!
H-- H'LO, MA'M!
DO **YOU** LIKE COWS? I KNOW YOUR **FRIEND** DOESN'T.
I DON'T LIKE TO **RIDE** 'EM, YOU OL' BAT!
FONE BONE **LOVES** COWS!
SORRY, DEAR. YOU CAN'T KEEP HIM.

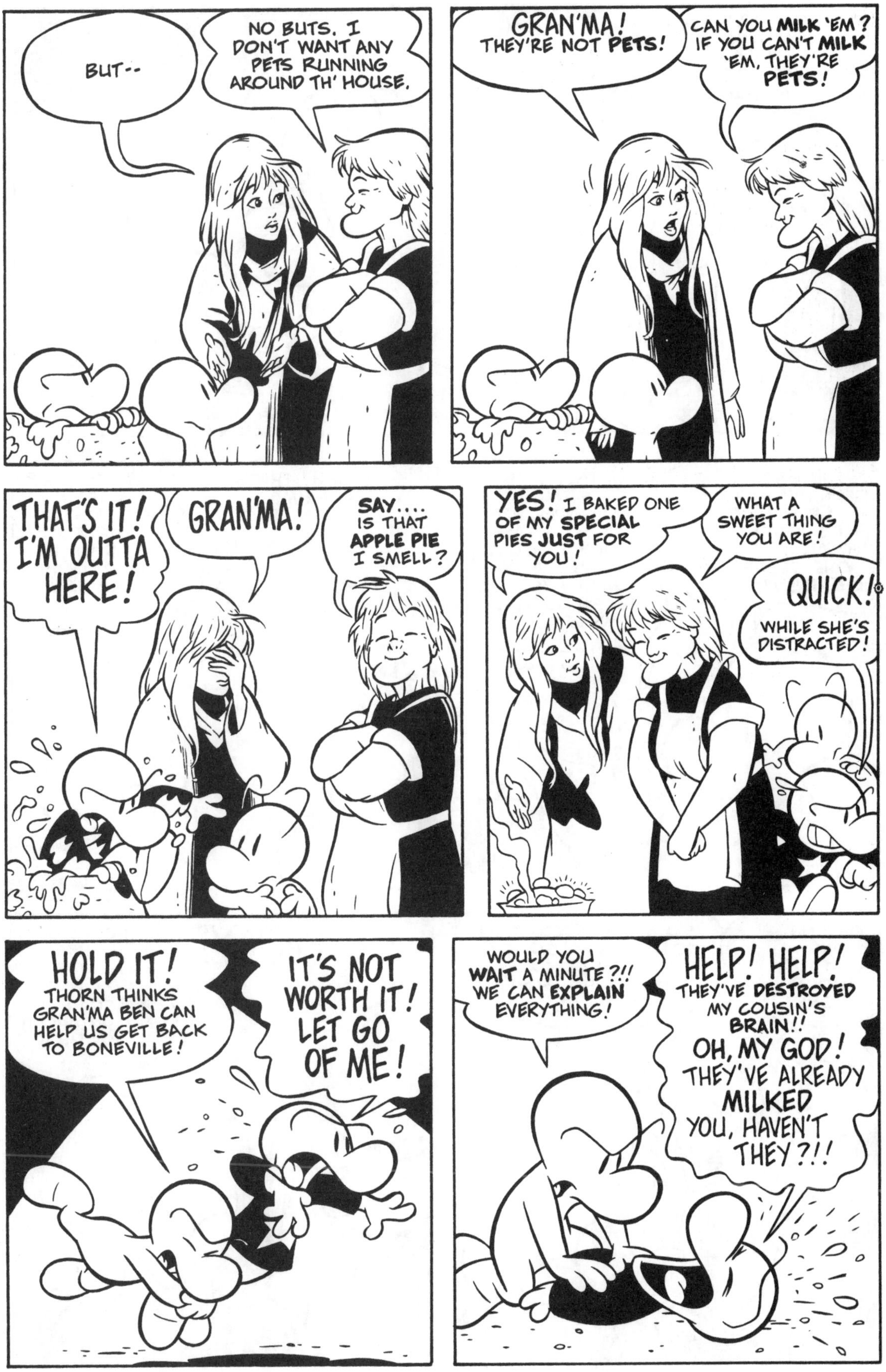
BUT--
NO BUTS. I DON'T WANT ANY PETS RUNNING AROUND TH' HOUSE.
GRAN'MA! THEY'RE NOT PETS!
CAN YOU MILK 'EM? IF YOU CAN'T MILK 'EM, THEY'RE PETS!
THAT'S IT! I'M OUTTA HERE!
GRAN'MA!
SAY.... IS THAT APPLE PIE I SMELL?
YES! I BAKED ONE OF MY SPECIAL PIES JUST FOR YOU!
WHAT A SWEET THING YOU ARE!
QUICK!
WHILE SHE'S DISTRACTED!
HOLD IT!
THORN THINKS GRAN'MA BEN CAN HELP US GET BACK TO BONEVILLE!
IT'S NOT WORTH IT! LET GO OF ME!
WOULD YOU WAIT A MINUTE?!! WE CAN EXPLAIN EVERYTHING!
HELP! HELP!
THEY'VE DESTROYED MY COUSIN'S BRAIN!!
OH, MY GOD!
THEY'VE ALREADY MILKED YOU, HAVEN'T THEY?!!

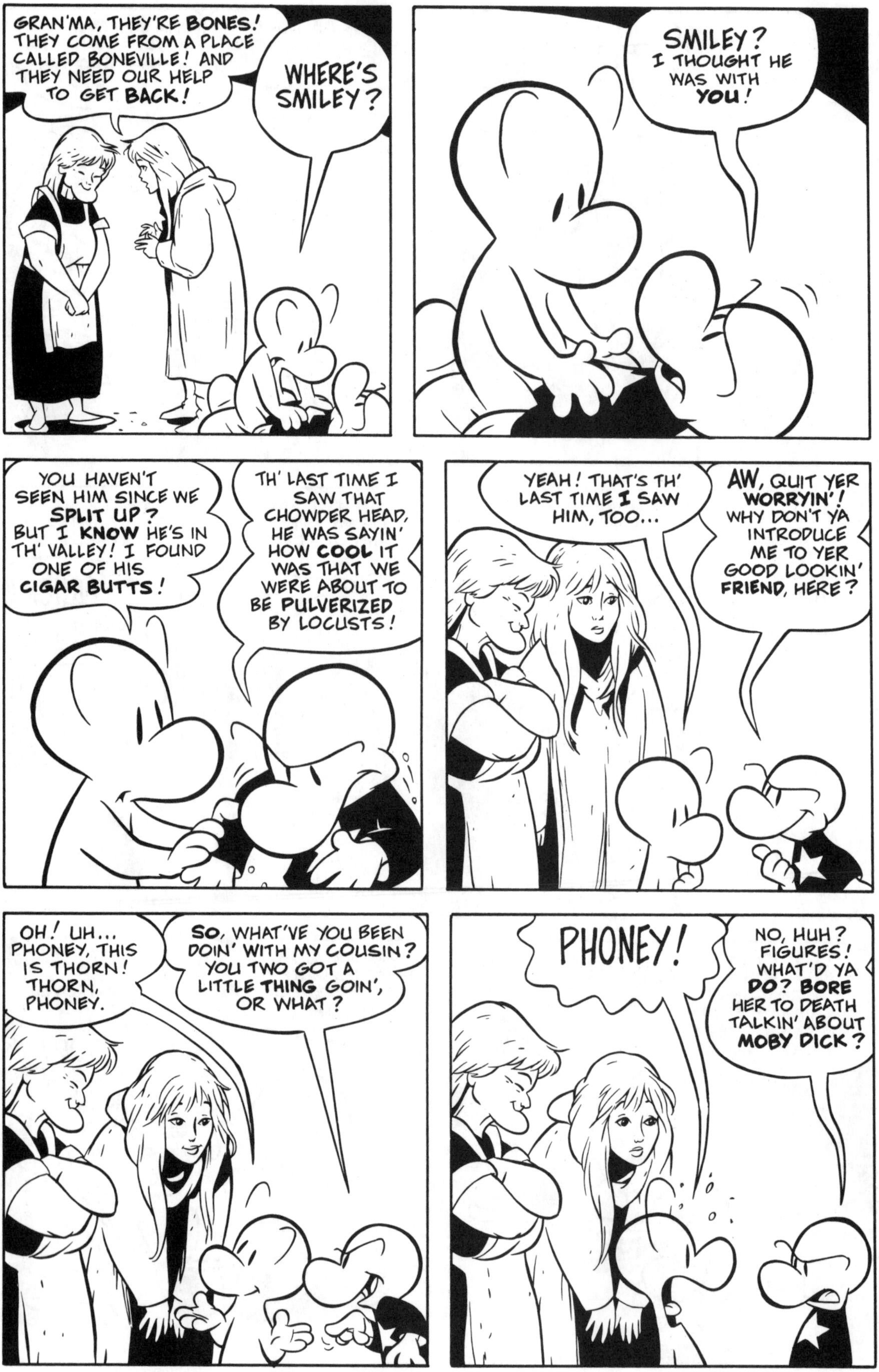
GRAN'MA, THEY'RE BONES! THEY COME FROM A PLACE CALLED BONEVILLE! AND THEY NEED OUR HELP TO GET BACK!
WHERE'S SMILEY?
SMILEY? I THOUGHT HE WAS WITH YOU!
YOU HAVEN'T SEEN HIM SINCE WE SPLIT UP? BUT I KNOW HE'S IN TH' VALLEY! I FOUND ONE OF HIS CIGAR BUTTS!
TH' LAST TIME I SAW THAT CHOWDER HEAD, HE WAS SAYIN' HOW COOL IT WAS THAT WE WERE ABOUT TO BE PULVERIZED BY LOCUSTS!
YEAH! THAT'S TH' LAST TIME I SAW HIM, TOO...
AW, QUIT YER WORRYIN'! WHY DON'T YA INTRODUCE ME TO YER GOOD LOOKIN' FRIEND, HERE?
OH! UH... PHONEY, THIS IS THORN! THORN, PHONEY.
SO, WHAT'VE YOU BEEN DOIN' WITH MY COUSIN? YOU TWO GOT A LITTLE THING GOIN', OR WHAT?
PHONEY!
NO, HUH? FIGURES! WHAT'D YA DO? BORE HER TO DEATH TALKIN' ABOUT MOBY DICK?

I'M GOING TO BED. YOU CAN KEEP 'EM IF YOU WANT, BUT THEY HAVE TO SLEEP IN TH' BARN.

GRAM!

G'NIGHT, MA'M! IT WAS NICE MEETING YOU!

FONE BONE, COULD I TALK TO YOU FOR A MOMENT? OUTSIDE?

YES.

WELL, GO AHEAD! I AIN'T STOPPIN' YA!

THIS ISN'T GOING QUITE THE WAY WE PLANNED, IS IT? TELL ME... IS HE ALWAYS LIKE THIS?

PRETTY MUCH.

HMM. GRAN'MA'S GOING BACK TO BARRELHAVEN IN A FEW DAYS FOR THE SPRING FESTIVAL. IF WE CAN JUST KEEP THOSE TWO CALM UNTIL THEN, WE CAN ALL GO INTO TOWN TOGETHER TO LOOK FOR YOUR OTHER COUSIN.

DON'T WORRY! I CAN HANDLE PHONEY!

GO BACK IN THE HOUSE AND KEEP AN EYE ON HIM. I HAVE TO GO GET SOME FRESH WATER FOR GRAN'MA TO WASH UP WITH...

OKAY, PHONEY! WE HAVE TO GET A COUPLE OF THINGS STRAIGHT---

Next: Barrelhaven

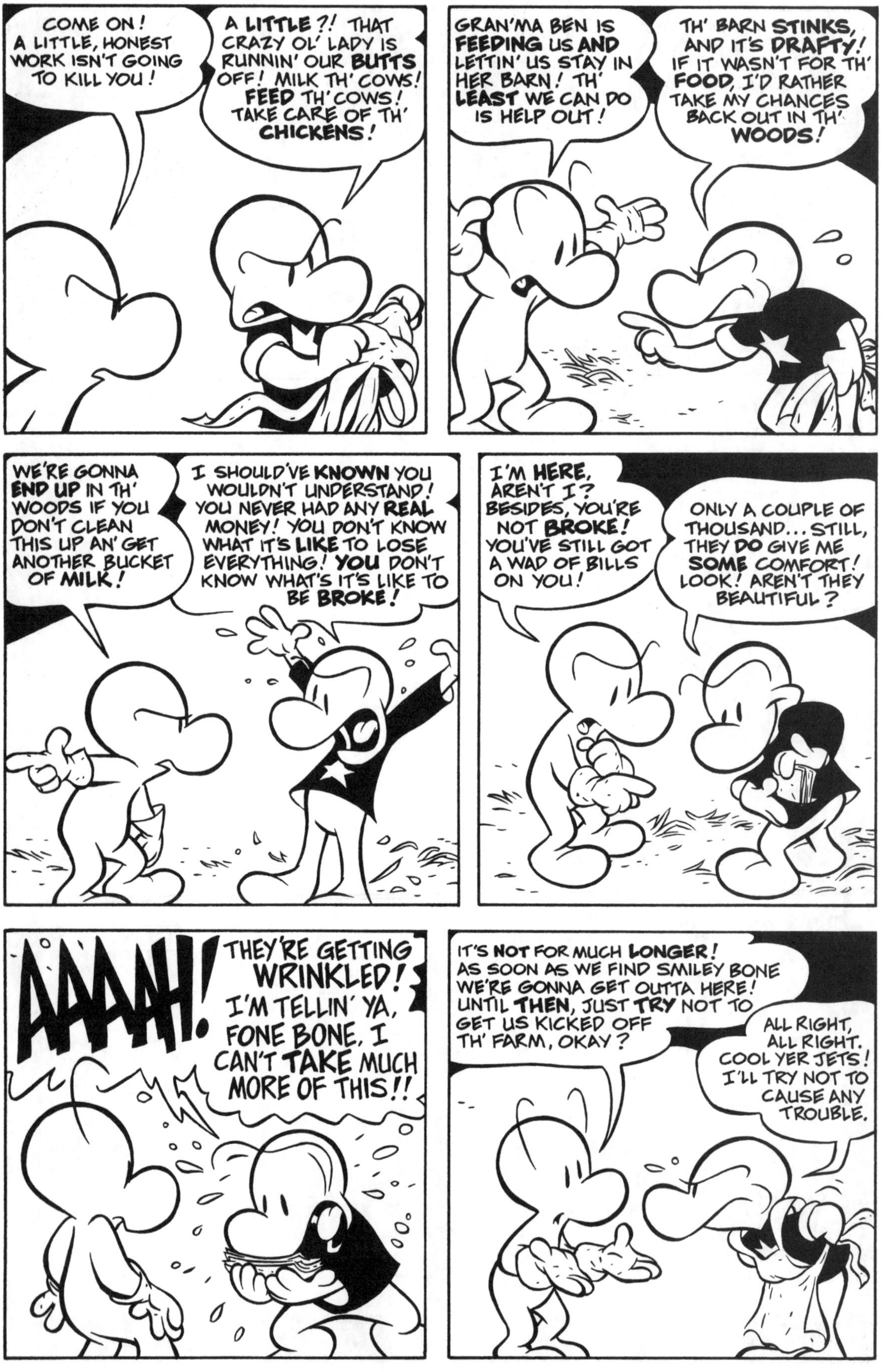
COME ON! A LITTLE, HONEST WORK ISN'T GOING TO KILL YOU!
A LITTLE?! THAT CRAZY OL' LADY IS RUNNIN' OUR BUTTS OFF! MILK TH' COWS! FEED TH' COWS! TAKE CARE OF TH' CHICKENS!
GRAN'MA BEN IS FEEDING US AND LETTIN' US STAY IN HER BARN! TH' LEAST WE CAN DO IS HELP OUT!
TH' BARN STINKS, AND IT'S DRAFTY! IF IT WASN'T FOR TH' FOOD, I'D RATHER TAKE MY CHANCES BACK OUT IN TH' WOODS!
WE'RE GONNA END UP IN TH' WOODS IF YOU DON'T CLEAN THIS UP AN' GET ANOTHER BUCKET OF MILK!
I SHOULD'VE KNOWN YOU WOULDN'T UNDERSTAND! YOU NEVER HAD ANY REAL MONEY! YOU DON'T KNOW WHAT IT'S LIKE TO LOSE EVERYTHING! YOU DON'T KNOW WHAT'S IT'S LIKE TO BE BROKE!
I'M HERE, AREN'T I? BESIDES, YOU'RE NOT BROKE! YOU'VE STILL GOT A WAD OF BILLS ON YOU!
ONLY A COUPLE OF THOUSAND... STILL, THEY DO GIVE ME SOME COMFORT! LOOK! AREN'T THEY BEAUTIFUL?
AAAAH!
THEY'RE GETTING WRINKLED! I'M TELLIN' YA, FONE BONE, I CAN'T TAKE MUCH MORE OF THIS!!
IT'S NOT FOR MUCH LONGER! AS SOON AS WE FIND SMILEY BONE WE'RE GONNA GET OUTTA HERE! UNTIL THEN, JUST TRY NOT TO GET US KICKED OFF TH' FARM, OKAY?
ALL RIGHT, ALL RIGHT. COOL YER JETS! I'LL TRY NOT TO CAUSE ANY TROUBLE.

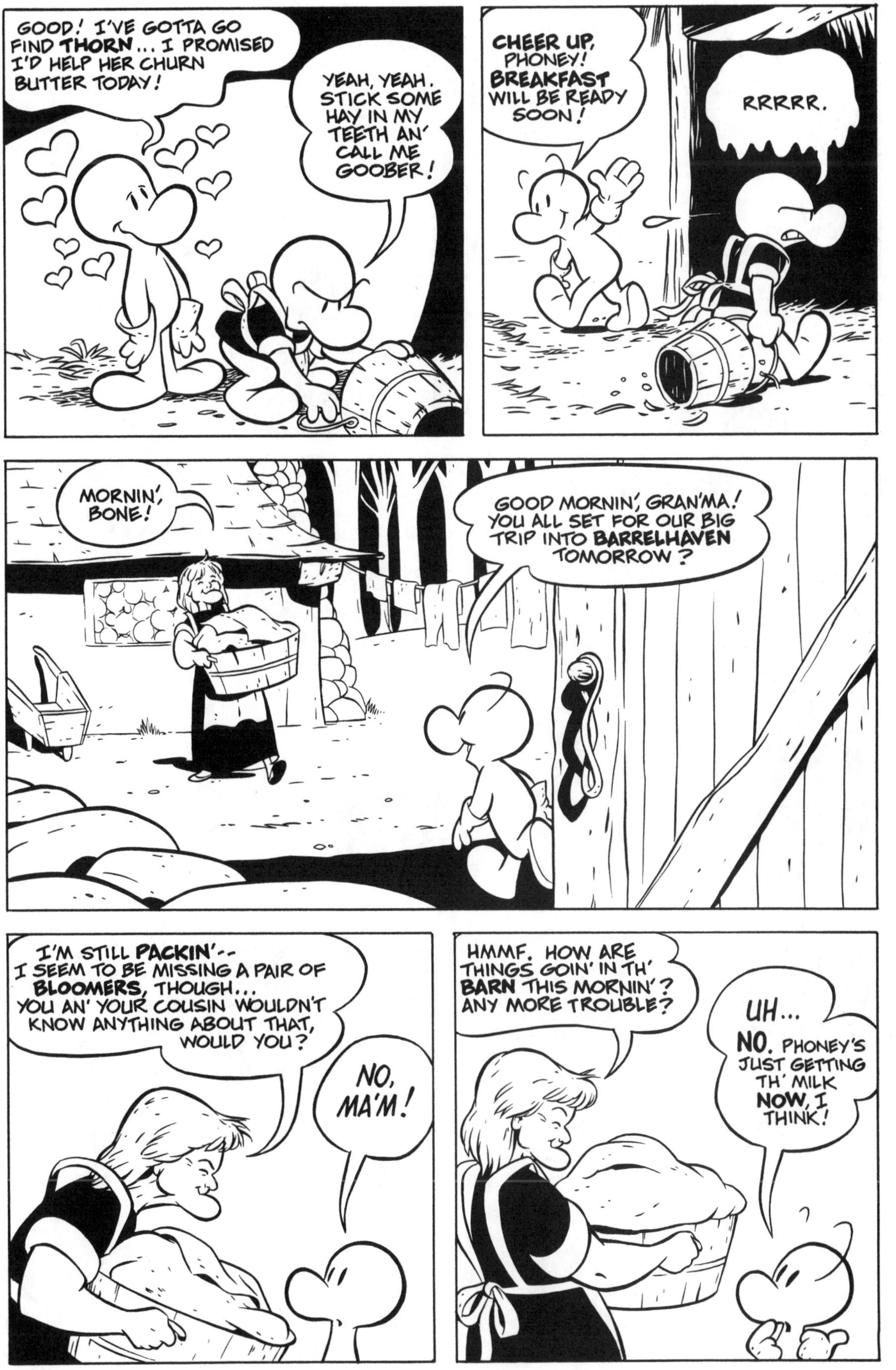
GOOD! I'VE GOTTA GO FIND THORN... I PROMISED I'D HELP HER CHURN BUTTER TODAY!
YEAH, YEAH. STICK SOME HAY IN MY TEETH AN' CALL ME GOOBER!
CHEER UP, PHONEY! BREAKFAST WILL BE READY SOON!
RRRRR.
MORNIN', BONE!
GOOD MORNIN', GRAN'MA! YOU ALL SET FOR OUR BIG TRIP INTO BARRELHAVEN TOMORROW?
I'M STILL PACKIN'-- I SEEM TO BE MISSING A PAIR OF BLOOMERS, THOUGH... YOU AN' YOUR COUSIN WOULDN'T KNOW ANYTHING ABOUT THAT, WOULD YOU?
NO, MA'M!
HMMF. HOW ARE THINGS GOIN' IN TH' BARN THIS MORNIN'? ANY MORE TROUBLE?
UH... NO. PHONEY'S JUST GETTING TH' MILK NOW, I THINK!

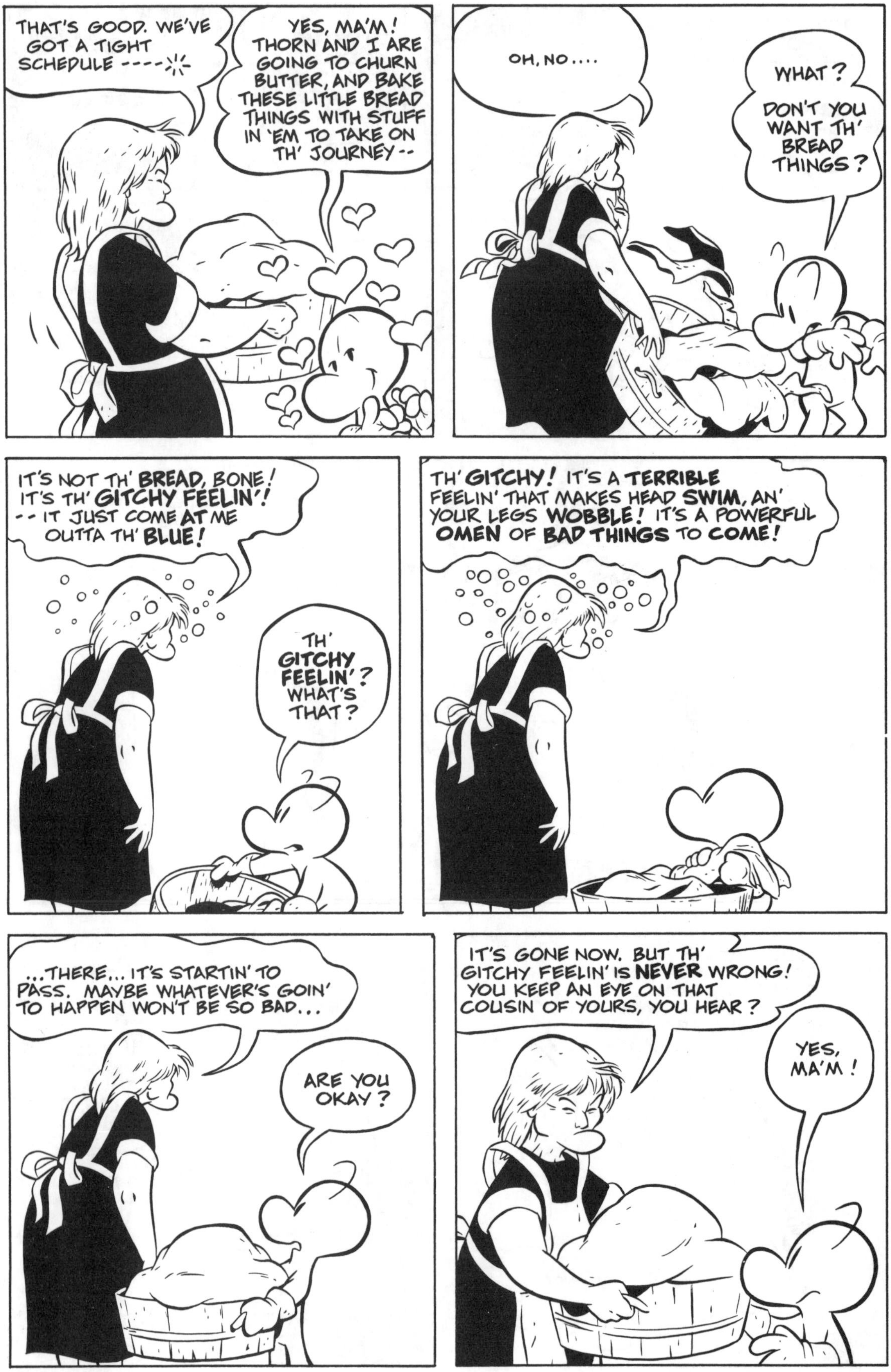
THAT'S GOOD. WE'VE GOT A TIGHT SCHEDULE ----
YES, MA'M! THORN AND I ARE GOING TO CHURN BUTTER, AND BAKE THESE LITTLE BREAD THINGS WITH STUFF IN 'EM TO TAKE ON TH' JOURNEY --
OH, NO....
WHAT? DON'T YOU WANT TH' BREAD THINGS?
IT'S NOT TH' BREAD, BONE! IT'S TH' GITCHY FEELIN'! -- IT JUST COME AT ME OUTTA TH' BLUE!
TH' GITCHY FEELIN'? WHAT'S THAT?
TH' GITCHY! IT'S A TERRIBLE FEELIN' THAT MAKES HEAD SWIM, AN' YOUR LEGS WOBBLE! IT'S A POWERFUL OMEN OF BAD THINGS TO COME!
...THERE... IT'S STARTIN' TO PASS. MAYBE WHATEVER'S GOIN' TO HAPPEN WON'T BE SO BAD...
ARE YOU OKAY?
IT'S GONE NOW. BUT TH' GITCHY FEELIN' IS NEVER WRONG! YOU KEEP AN EYE ON THAT COUSIN OF YOURS, YOU HEAR?
YES, MA'M!

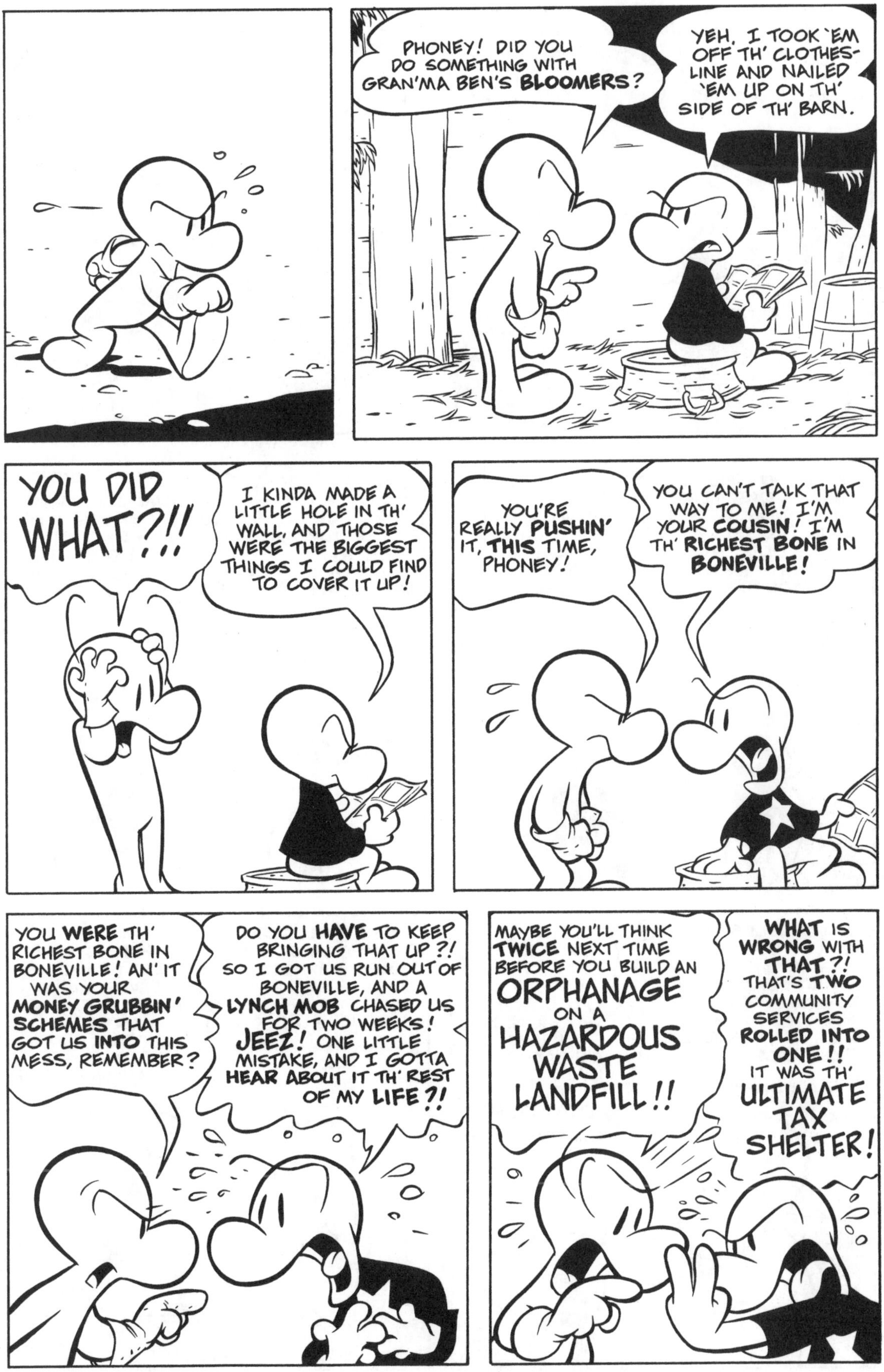

PHONEY! DID YOU DO SOMETHING WITH GRAN'MA BEN'S BLOOMERS?
YEH. I TOOK 'EM OFF TH' CLOTHES-LINE AND NAILED 'EM UP ON TH' SIDE OF TH' BARN.
YOU DID WHAT?!!
I KINDA MADE A LITTLE HOLE IN TH' WALL, AND THOSE WERE THE BIGGEST THINGS I COULD FIND TO COVER IT UP!
YOU'RE REALLY PUSHIN' IT, THIS TIME, PHONEY!
YOU CAN'T TALK THAT WAY TO ME! I'M YOUR COUSIN! I'M TH' RICHEST BONE IN BONEVILLE!
YOU WERE TH' RICHEST BONE IN BONEVILLE! AN' IT WAS YOUR MONEY GRUBBIN' SCHEMES THAT GOT US INTO THIS MESS, REMEMBER?
DO YOU HAVE TO KEEP BRINGING THAT UP?! SO I GOT US RUN OUT OF BONEVILLE, AND A LYNCH MOB CHASED US FOR TWO WEEKS! JEEZ! ONE LITTLE MISTAKE, AND I GOTTA HEAR ABOUT IT TH' REST OF MY LIFE?!
MAYBE YOU'LL THINK TWICE NEXT TIME BEFORE YOU BUILD AN ORPHANAGE ON A HAZARDOUS WASTE LANDFILL!!
WHAT IS WRONG WITH THAT?! THAT'S TWO COMMUNITY SERVICES ROLLED INTO ONE!! IT WAS TH' ULTIMATE TAX SHELTER!

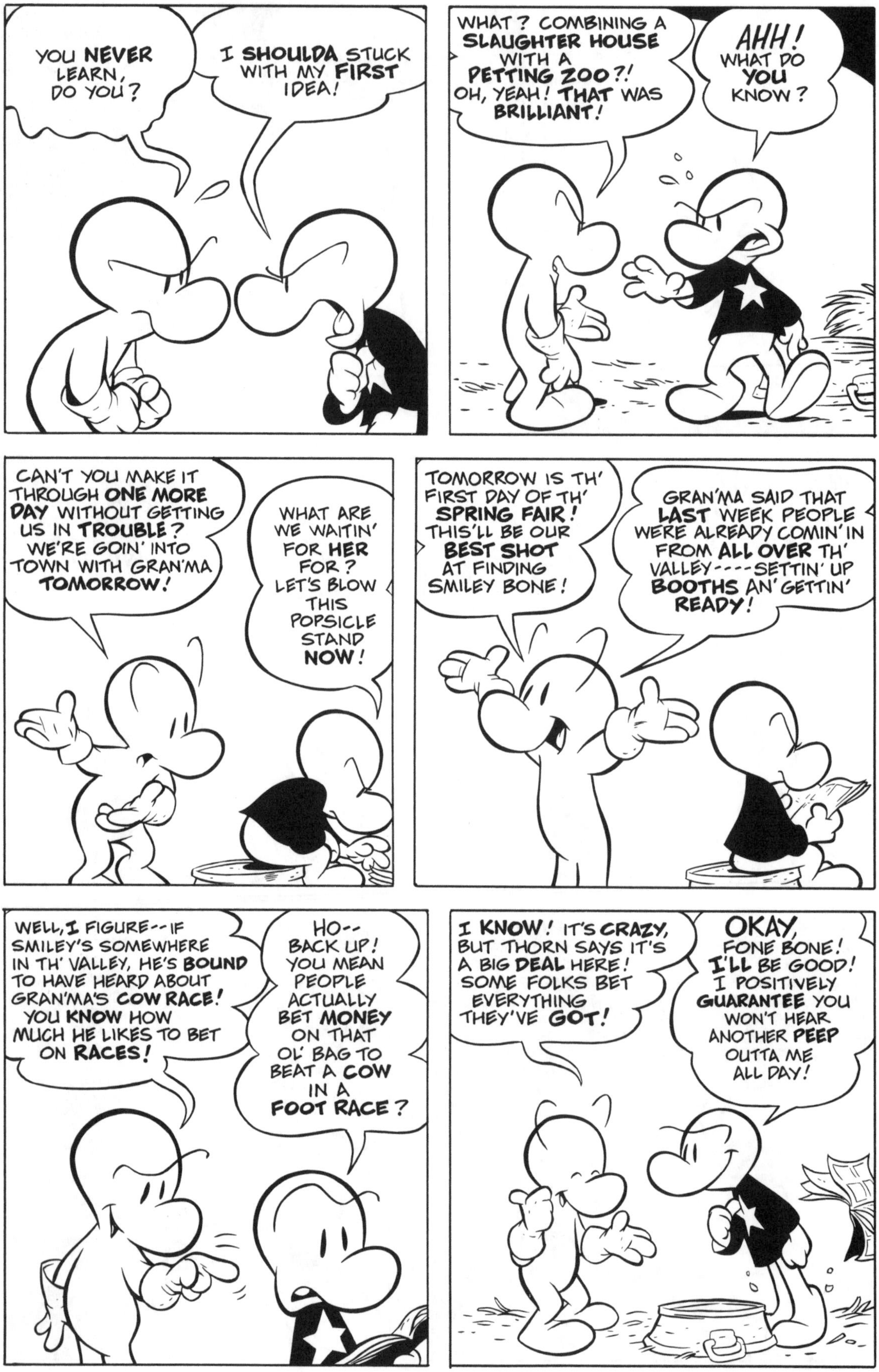

YOU NEVER LEARN, DO YOU?
I SHOULDA STUCK WITH MY FIRST IDEA!
WHAT? COMBINING A SLAUGHTER HOUSE WITH A PETTING ZOO?! OH, YEAH! THAT WAS BRILLIANT!
AHH! WHAT DO YOU KNOW?
CAN'T YOU MAKE IT THROUGH ONE MORE DAY WITHOUT GETTING US IN TROUBLE? WE'RE GOIN' INTO TOWN WITH GRAN'MA TOMORROW!
WHAT ARE WE WAITIN' FOR HER FOR? LET'S BLOW THIS POPSICLE STAND NOW!
TOMORROW IS TH' FIRST DAY OF TH' SPRING FAIR! THIS'LL BE OUR BEST SHOT AT FINDING SMILEY BONE!
GRAN'MA SAID THAT LAST WEEK PEOPLE WERE ALREADY COMIN' IN FROM ALL OVER TH' VALLEY----SETTIN' UP BOOTHS AN' GETTIN' READY!
WELL, I FIGURE--IF SMILEY'S SOMEWHERE IN TH' VALLEY, HE'S BOUND TO HAVE HEARD ABOUT GRAN'MA'S COW RACE! YOU KNOW HOW MUCH HE LIKES TO BET ON RACES!
HO--BACK UP! YOU MEAN PEOPLE ACTUALLY BET MONEY ON THAT OL' BAG TO BEAT A COW IN A FOOT RACE?
I KNOW! IT'S CRAZY, BUT THORN SAYS IT'S A BIG DEAL HERE! SOME FOLKS BET EVERYTHING THEY'VE GOT!
OKAY, FONE BONE! I'LL BE GOOD! I POSITIVELY GUARANTEE YOU WON'T HEAR ANOTHER PEEP OUTTA ME ALL DAY!

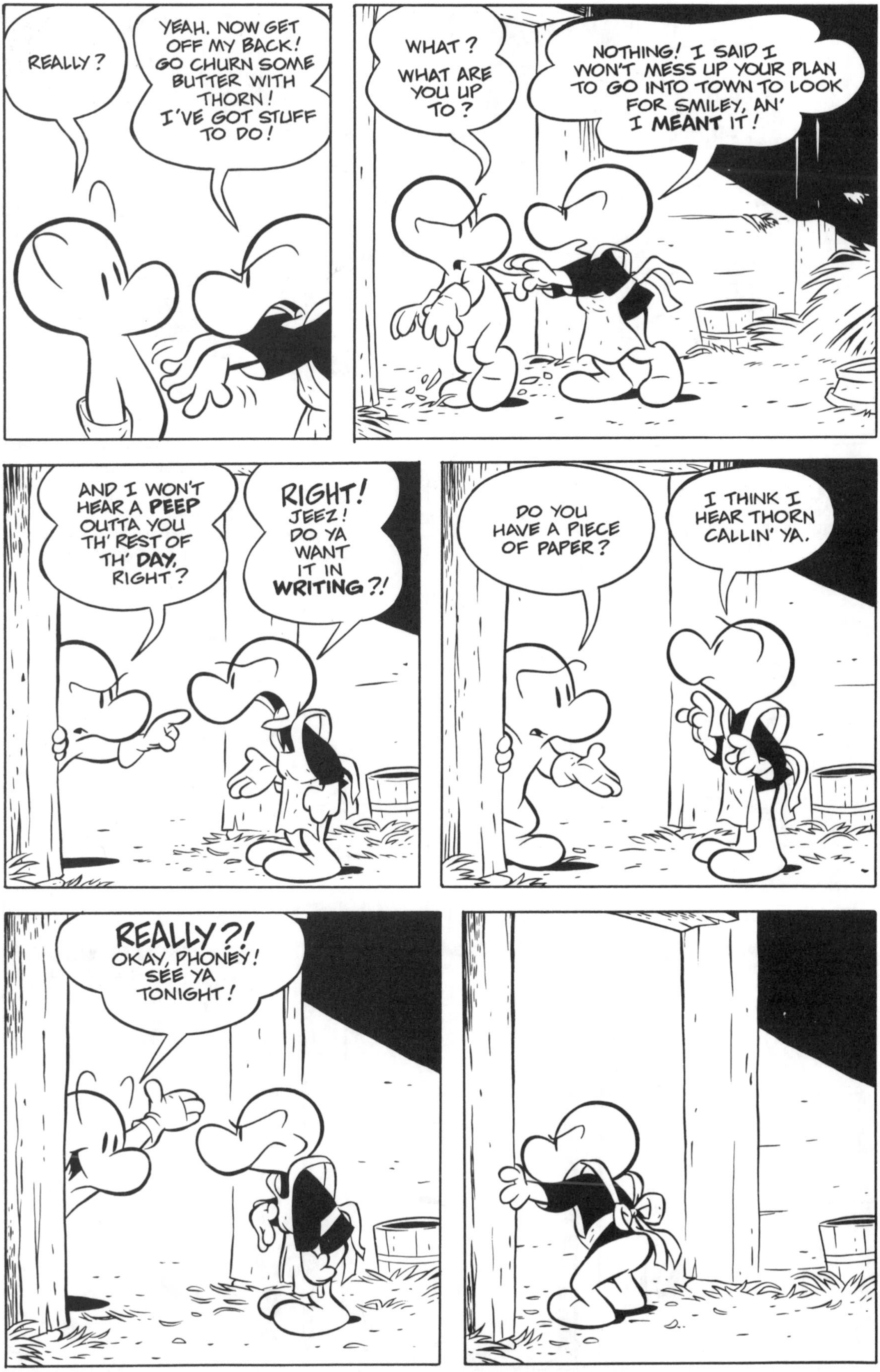
REALLY?
YEAH. NOW GET OFF MY BACK! GO CHURN SOME BUTTER WITH THORN! I'VE GOT STUFF TO DO!
WHAT? WHAT ARE YOU UP TO?
NOTHING! I SAID I WON'T MESS UP YOUR PLAN TO GO INTO TOWN TO LOOK FOR SMILEY, AN' I MEANT IT!
AND I WON'T HEAR A PEEP OUTTA YOU TH' REST OF TH' DAY, RIGHT?
RIGHT! JEEZ! DO YA WANT IT IN WRITING?!
DO YOU HAVE A PIECE OF PAPER?
I THINK I HEAR THORN CALLIN' YA.
REALLY?! OKAY, PHONEY! SEE YA TONIGHT!

YEP, YOU WON'T HEAR A **PEEP** OUTTA **ME**, 'CAUSE **I** AIN'T GONNA **BE** HERE!

FONE BONE WON'T MIND IF I BORROW A FEW OF HIS THINGS.... I MIGHT NEED 'EM ON MY WAY TO TOWN....

SOUNDS LIKE A LOTTA **MONEY'S** GONNA CHANGE HANDS TOMORROW, AN' I DON'T SEE WHY GRAN'MA BEN SHOULD **HOG** IT ALL!

NO, SIRREE! IF THERE'S **BOOKMAKIN'** TO BE DONE, **I'M** TH' MAN TO **DO** IT!

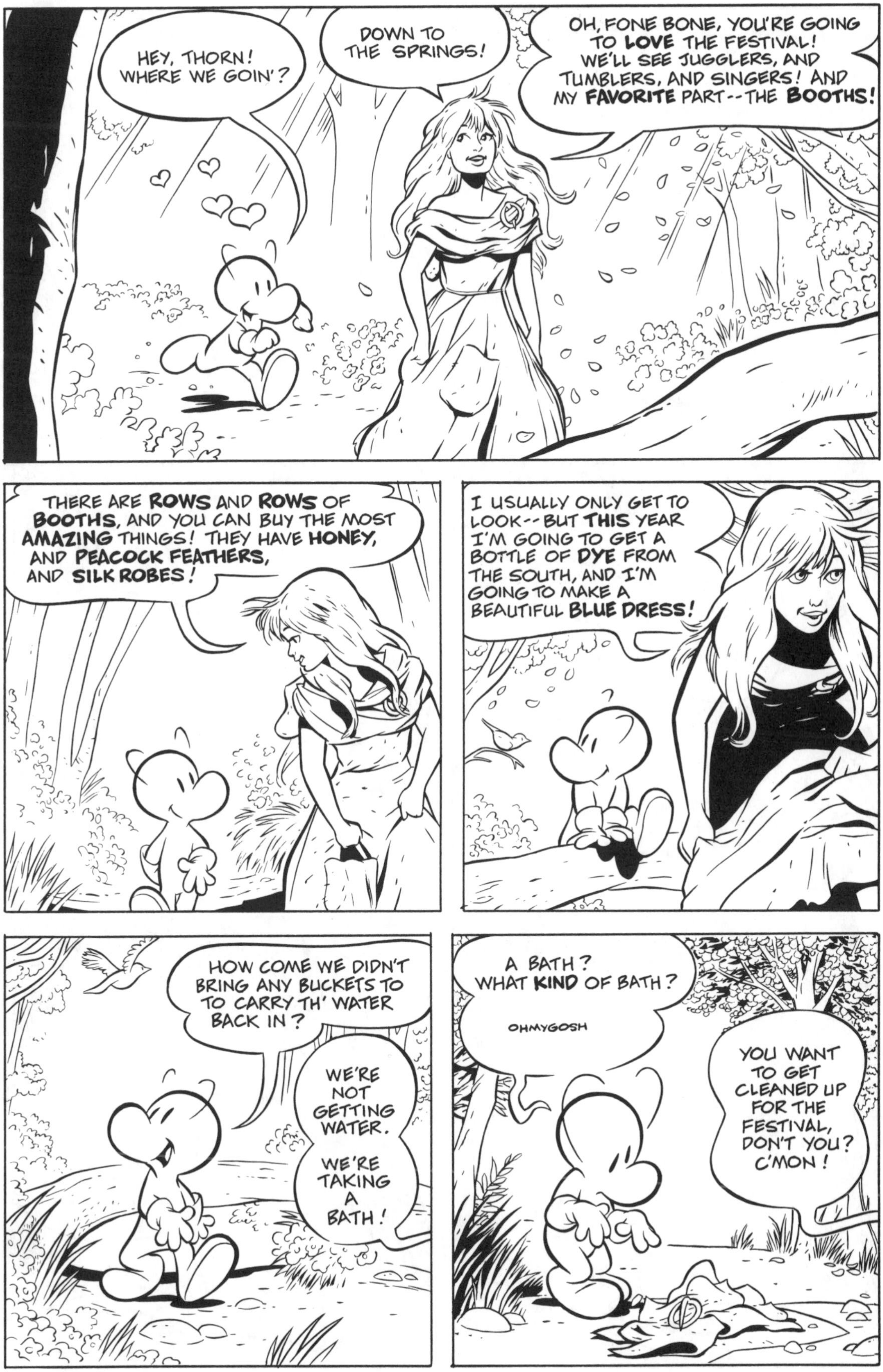
HEY, THORN! WHERE WE GOIN'?
DOWN TO THE SPRINGS!
OH, FONE BONE, YOU'RE GOING TO LOVE THE FESTIVAL! WE'LL SEE JUGGLERS, AND TUMBLERS, AND SINGERS! AND MY FAVORITE PART--THE BOOTHS!
THERE ARE ROWS AND ROWS OF BOOTHS, AND YOU CAN BUY THE MOST AMAZING THINGS! THEY HAVE HONEY, AND PEACOCK FEATHERS, AND SILK ROBES!
I USUALLY ONLY GET TO LOOK--BUT THIS YEAR I'M GOING TO GET A BOTTLE OF DYE FROM THE SOUTH, AND I'M GOING TO MAKE A BEAUTIFUL BLUE DRESS!
HOW COME WE DIDN'T BRING ANY BUCKETS TO TO CARRY TH' WATER BACK IN?
WE'RE NOT GETTING WATER.
WE'RE TAKING A BATH!
A BATH? WHAT KIND OF BATH?
OHMYGOSH
YOU WANT TO GET CLEANED UP FOR THE FESTIVAL, DON'T YOU? C'MON!

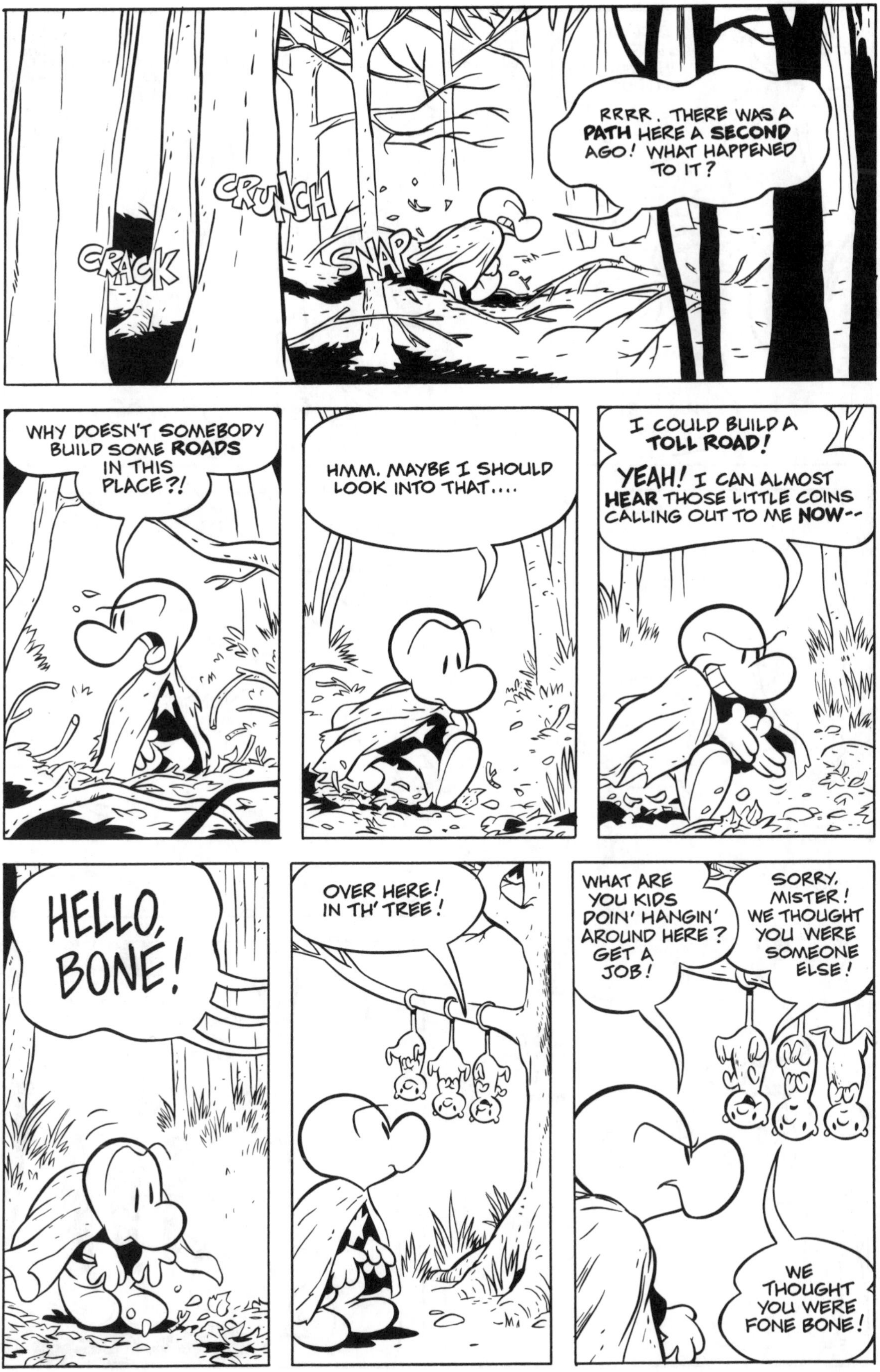
CRACK
CRUNCH
SNAP
RRRR. THERE WAS A PATH HERE A SECOND AGO! WHAT HAPPENED TO IT?
WHY DOESN'T SOMEBODY BUILD SOME ROADS IN THIS PLACE?!
HMM. MAYBE I SHOULD LOOK INTO THAT....
I COULD BUILD A TOLL ROAD!
YEAH! I CAN ALMOST HEAR THOSE LITTLE COINS CALLING OUT TO ME NOW--
HELLO, BONE!
OVER HERE! IN TH' TREE!
WHAT ARE YOU KIDS DOIN' HANGIN' AROUND HERE? GET A JOB!
SORRY, MISTER! WE THOUGHT YOU WERE SOMEONE ELSE!
WE THOUGHT YOU WERE FONE BONE!

I'M HIS COUSIN.

HIS **COUSIN**? ALL **RIGHT**! YOU WANNA PLAY WITH US?

WE'RE LEARNIN' HOW TO HANG BY OUR TAILS!

NO, THANKS. I'M ON MY WAY INTO TOWN.

HEY, MISTER! YOU KNOW TH' **WAY** INTO TOWN?

YEAH. WHY?

IT'S **THAT** WAY.

OH! RIGHT!

THANKS, KID! WHEN I COME BACK, I'LL BRING YOU A **CARROT**!

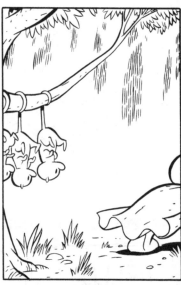

A CARROT? WHAT'S HE THINK WE ARE? RABBITS?

WHAT A DORK.

LUCKY THING I RAN INTO THOSE KIDS! AS SOON AS I'M BACK ON TH' RIGHT PATH, I SHOULD GET TO BARRELHAVEN IN **NO TIME**!

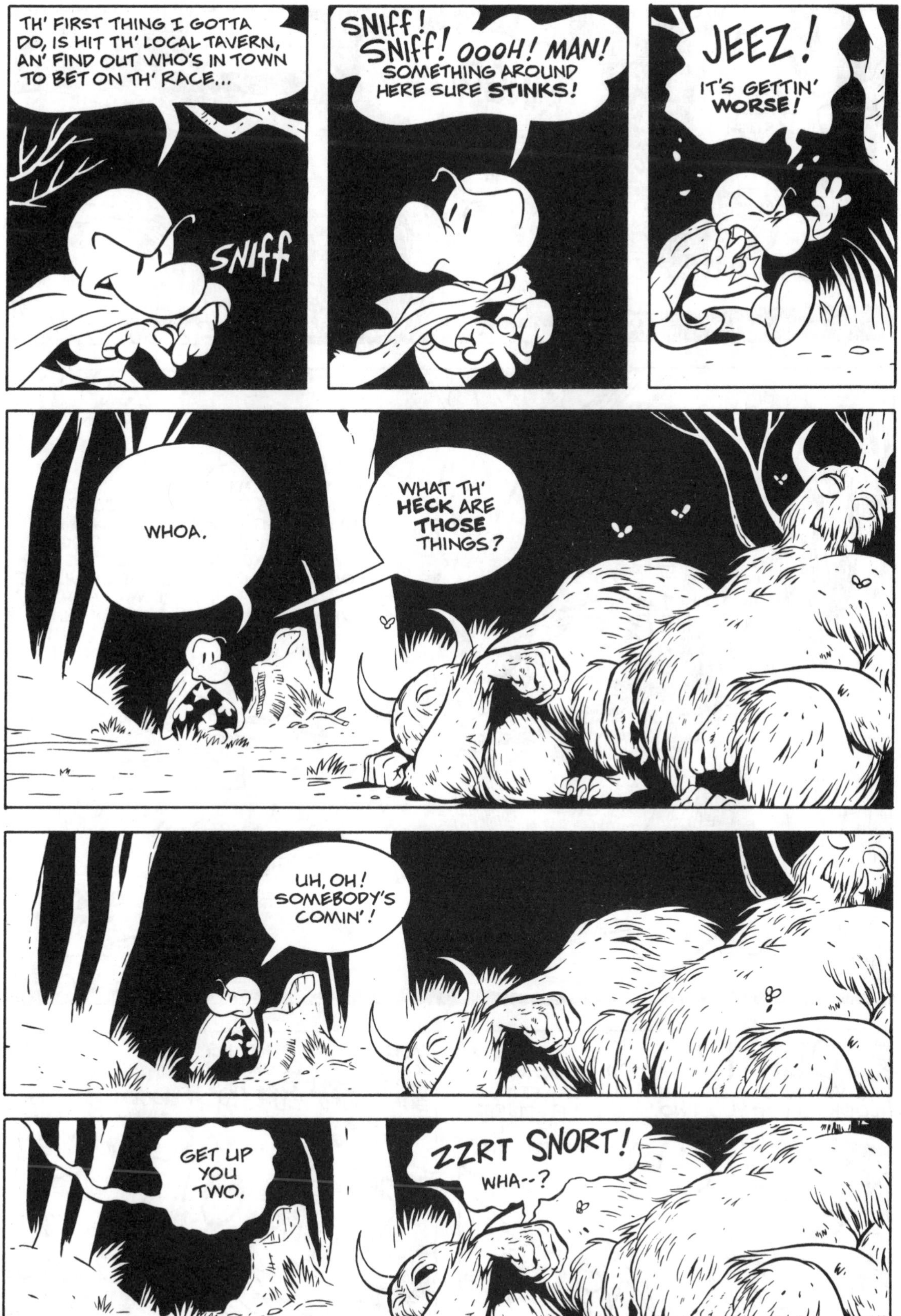
TH' FIRST THING I GOTTA DO, IS HIT TH' LOCAL TAVERN, AN' FIND OUT WHO'S IN TOWN TO BET ON TH' RACE...
SNIFF
SNIFF! SNIFF! OOOH! MAN! SOMETHING AROUND HERE SURE STINKS!
JEEZ! IT'S GETTIN' WORSE!
WHOA.
WHAT TH' HECK ARE THOSE THINGS?
UH, OH! SOMEBODY'S COMIN'!
GET UP YOU TWO.
ZZRT SNORT! WHA--?

GET UP BEFORE I CRUSH YOUR HEADS.

KINGDOK!

KINGDOK?

SIRE! WHAT ARE **YOU** DOING HERE? MAY I KISS YOUR FEET? I WISH I HAD SOME **QUICHE** I COULD OFFER YOU--

W-WOULD YOU LIKE SOME OF THE SMALL DEAD THING I FOUND UNDER A BUSH? I WAS SAVING? HALF FOR LATER, BUT YOU'RE MORE THAN WELCOME--

QUIET! I'VE HAD SCOUTS OUT LOOKING FOR YOU TWO!

Y-YOU HAVE? HOW FLATTERING! I'M FLATTERED! ARE YOU FLATTERED?

YOU TWO ARE STARTING TO MAKE ME LOOK BAD. THE **HOODED ONE** HAS SUMMONED YOU BOTH TO A HIGH COUNCIL-- **TONIGHT**!

THE HOODED ONE--

HAS SOMETHING HAPPENED?

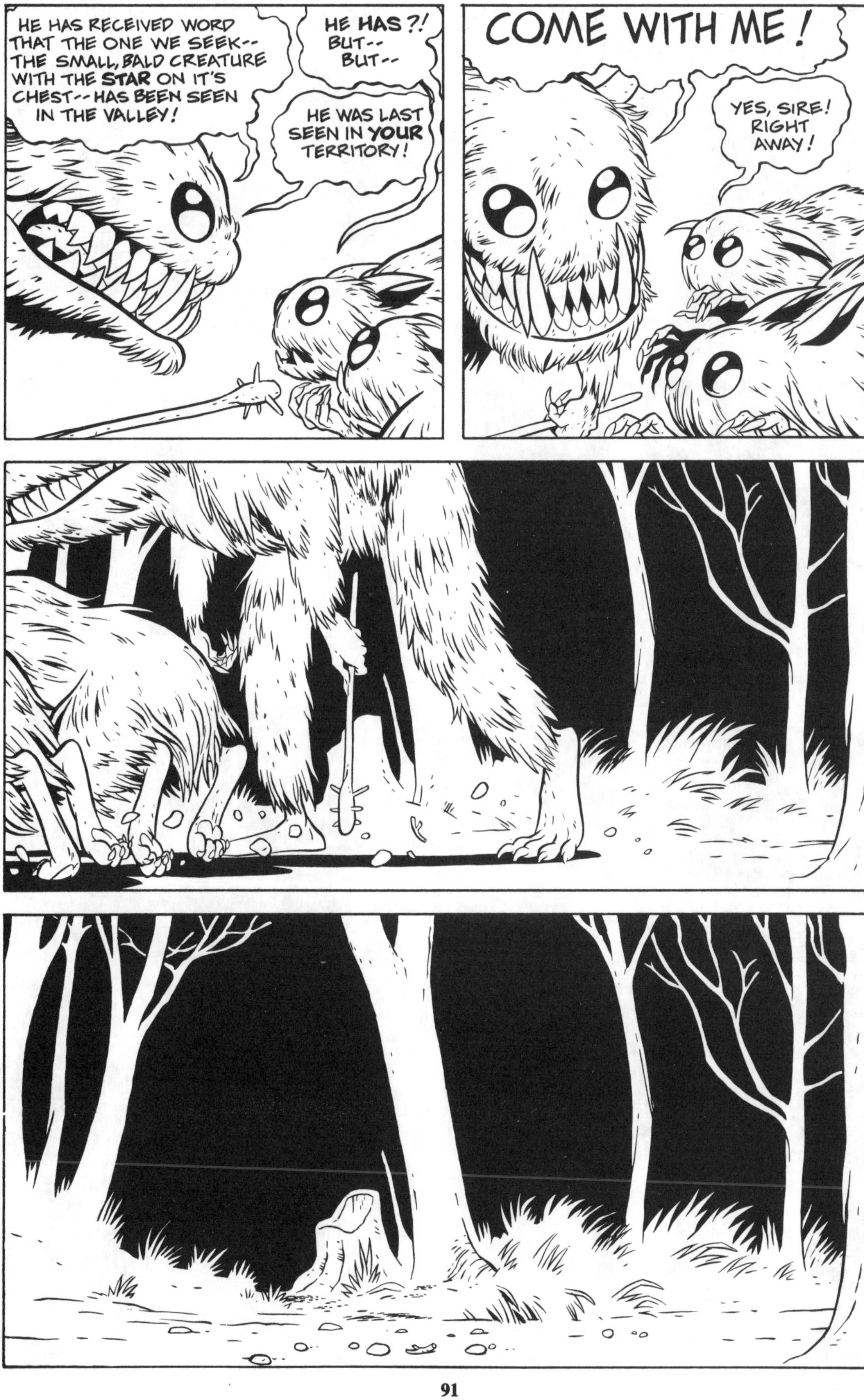
HE HAS RECEIVED WORD THAT THE ONE WE SEEK-- THE SMALL, BALD CREATURE WITH THE STAR ON IT'S CHEST--HAS BEEN SEEN IN THE VALLEY!
HE HAS?! BUT-- BUT--
HE WAS LAST SEEN IN YOUR TERRITORY!
COME WITH ME!
YES, SIRE! RIGHT AWAY!

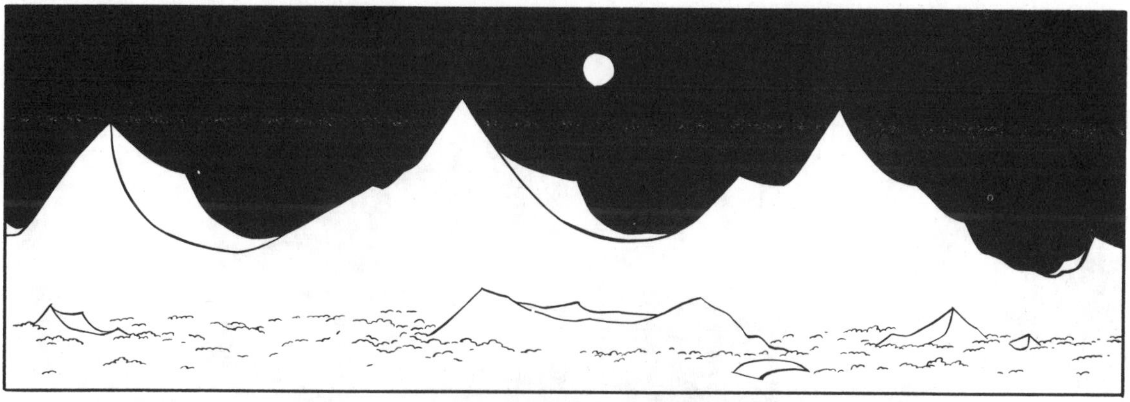

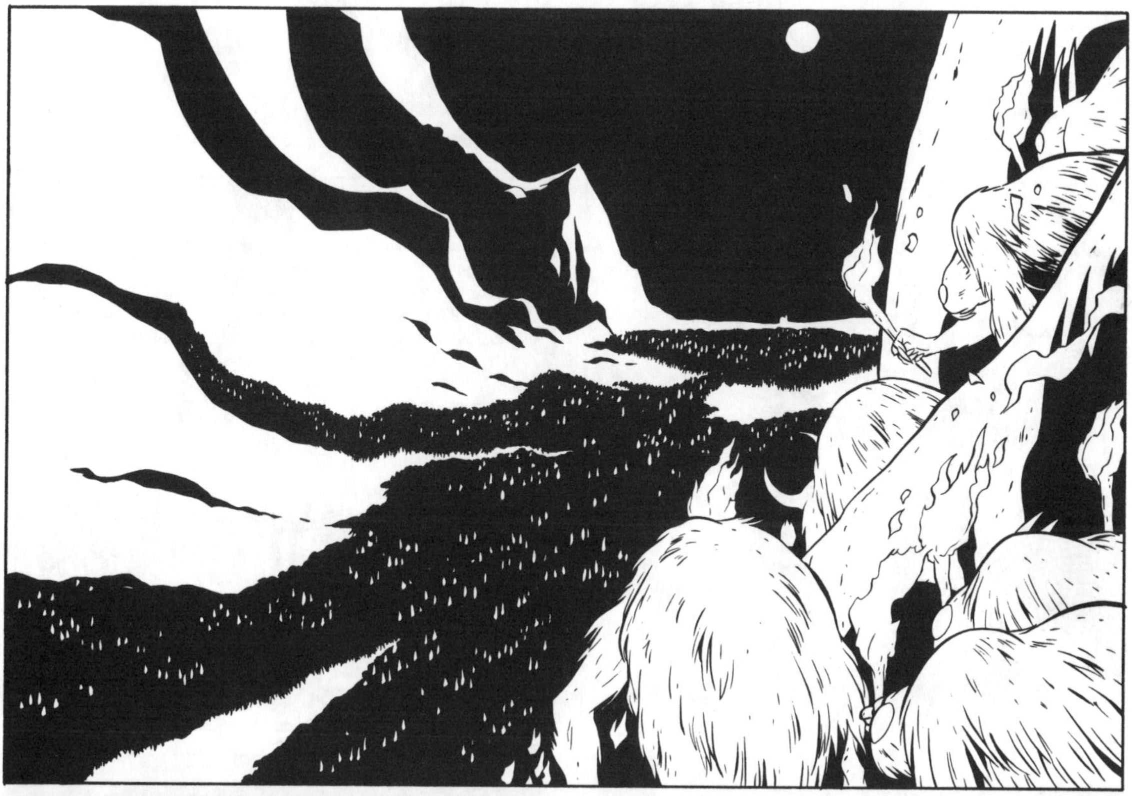

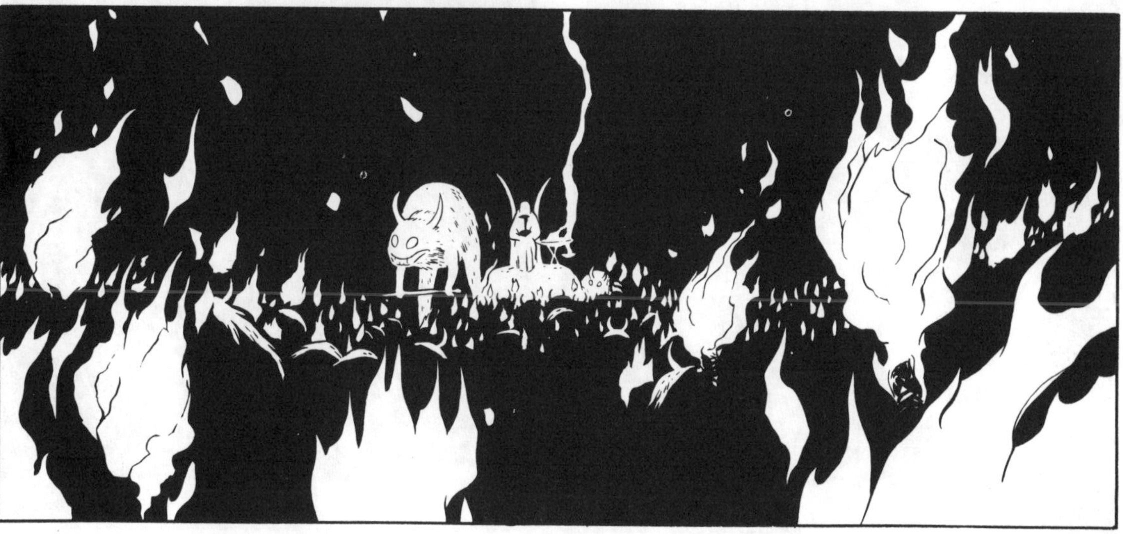

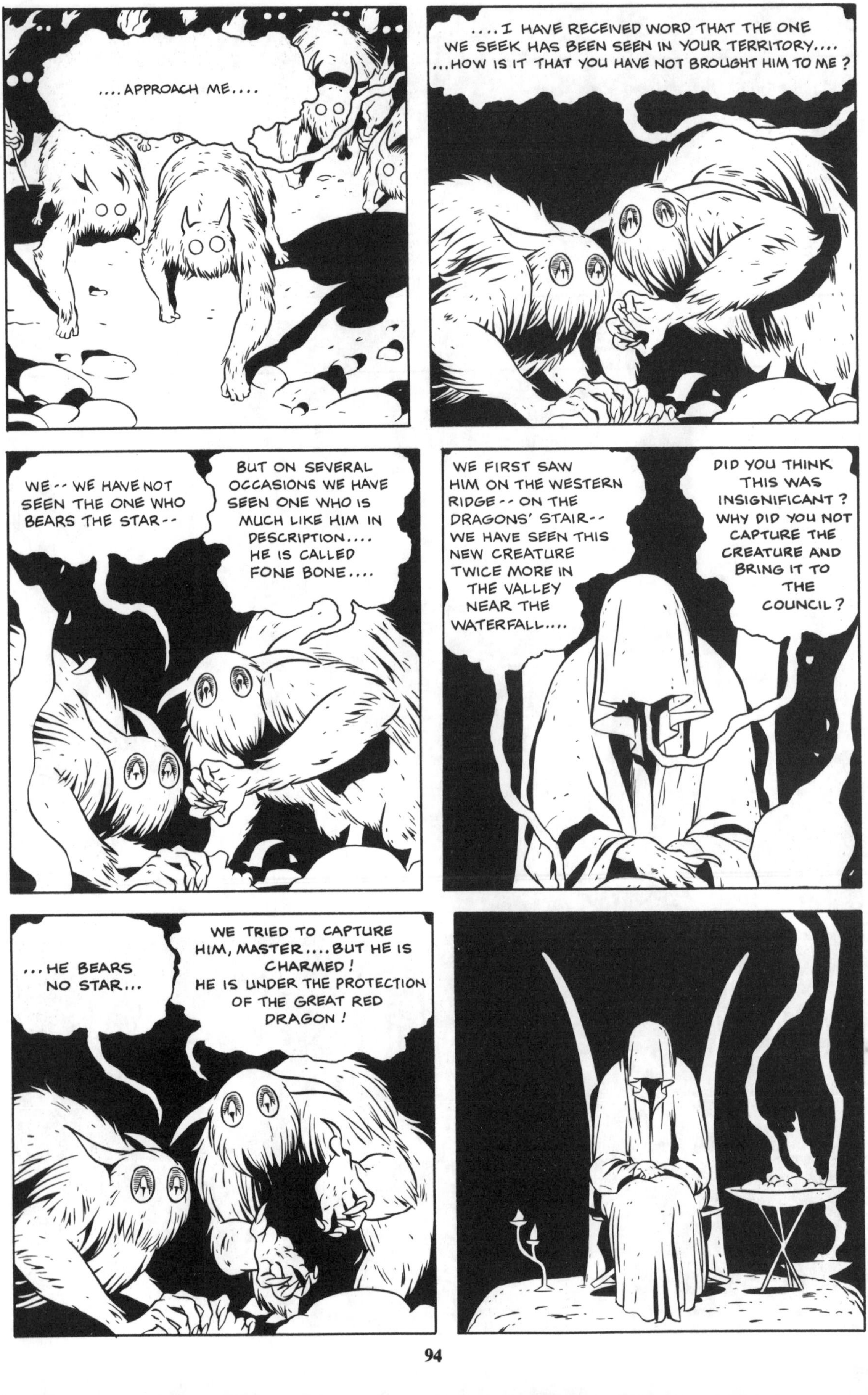
....APPROACH ME....
....I HAVE RECEIVED WORD THAT THE ONE WE SEEK HAS BEEN SEEN IN YOUR TERRITORY.... ...HOW IS IT THAT YOU HAVE NOT BROUGHT HIM TO ME?
WE-- WE HAVE NOT SEEN THE ONE WHO BEARS THE STAR--
BUT ON SEVERAL OCCASIONS WE HAVE SEEN ONE WHO IS MUCH LIKE HIM IN DESCRIPTION.... HE IS CALLED FONE BONE....
WE FIRST SAW HIM ON THE WESTERN RIDGE-- ON THE DRAGONS' STAIR-- WE HAVE SEEN THIS NEW CREATURE TWICE MORE IN THE VALLEY NEAR THE WATERFALL....
DID YOU THINK THIS WAS INSIGNIFICANT? WHY DID YOU NOT CAPTURE THE CREATURE AND BRING IT TO THE COUNCIL?
...HE BEARS NO STAR...
WE TRIED TO CAPTURE HIM, MASTER....BUT HE IS CHARMED! HE IS UNDER THE PROTECTION OF THE GREAT RED DRAGON!

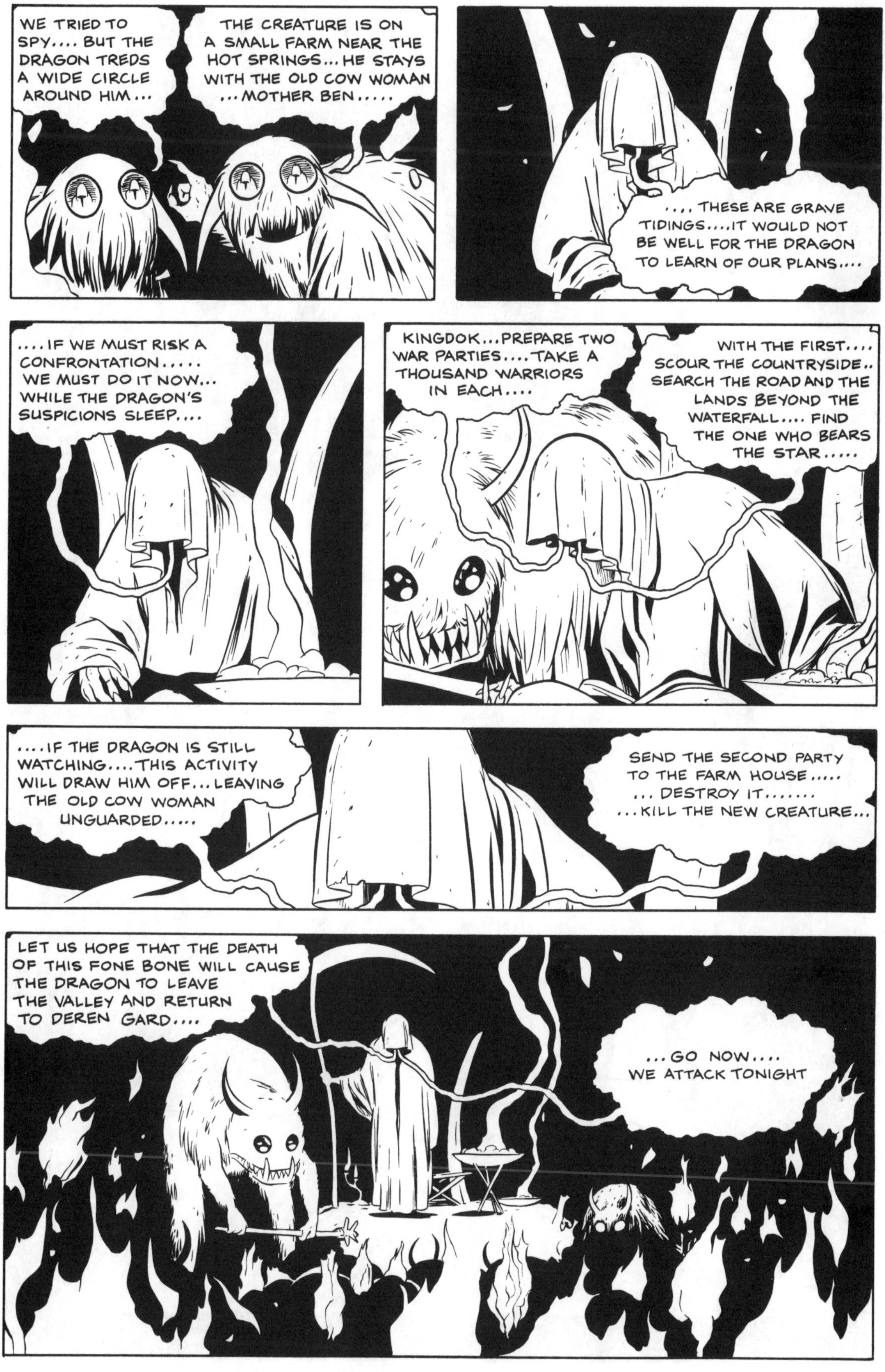
WE TRIED TO SPY.... BUT THE DRAGON TREDS A WIDE CIRCLE AROUND HIM...
THE CREATURE IS ON A SMALL FARM NEAR THE HOT SPRINGS... HE STAYS WITH THE OLD COW WOMAN ...MOTHER BEN.....
.... THESE ARE GRAVE TIDINGS....IT WOULD NOT BE WELL FOR THE DRAGON TO LEARN OF OUR PLANS....
....IF WE MUST RISK A CONFRONTATION..... WE MUST DO IT NOW... WHILE THE DRAGON'S SUSPICIONS SLEEP....
KINGDOK...PREPARE TWO WAR PARTIES....TAKE A THOUSAND WARRIORS IN EACH....
WITH THE FIRST.... SCOUR THE COUNTRYSIDE.. SEARCH THE ROAD AND THE LANDS BEYOND THE WATERFALL.... FIND THE ONE WHO BEARS THE STAR.....
....IF THE DRAGON IS STILL WATCHING....THIS ACTIVITY WILL DRAW HIM OFF...LEAVING THE OLD COW WOMAN UNGUARDED.....
SEND THE SECOND PARTY TO THE FARM HOUSE..... ... DESTROY IT....... ...KILL THE NEW CREATURE...
LET US HOPE THAT THE DEATH OF THIS FONE BONE WILL CAUSE THE DRAGON TO LEAVE THE VALLEY AND RETURN TO DEREN GARD....
...GO NOW.... WE ATTACK TONIGHT

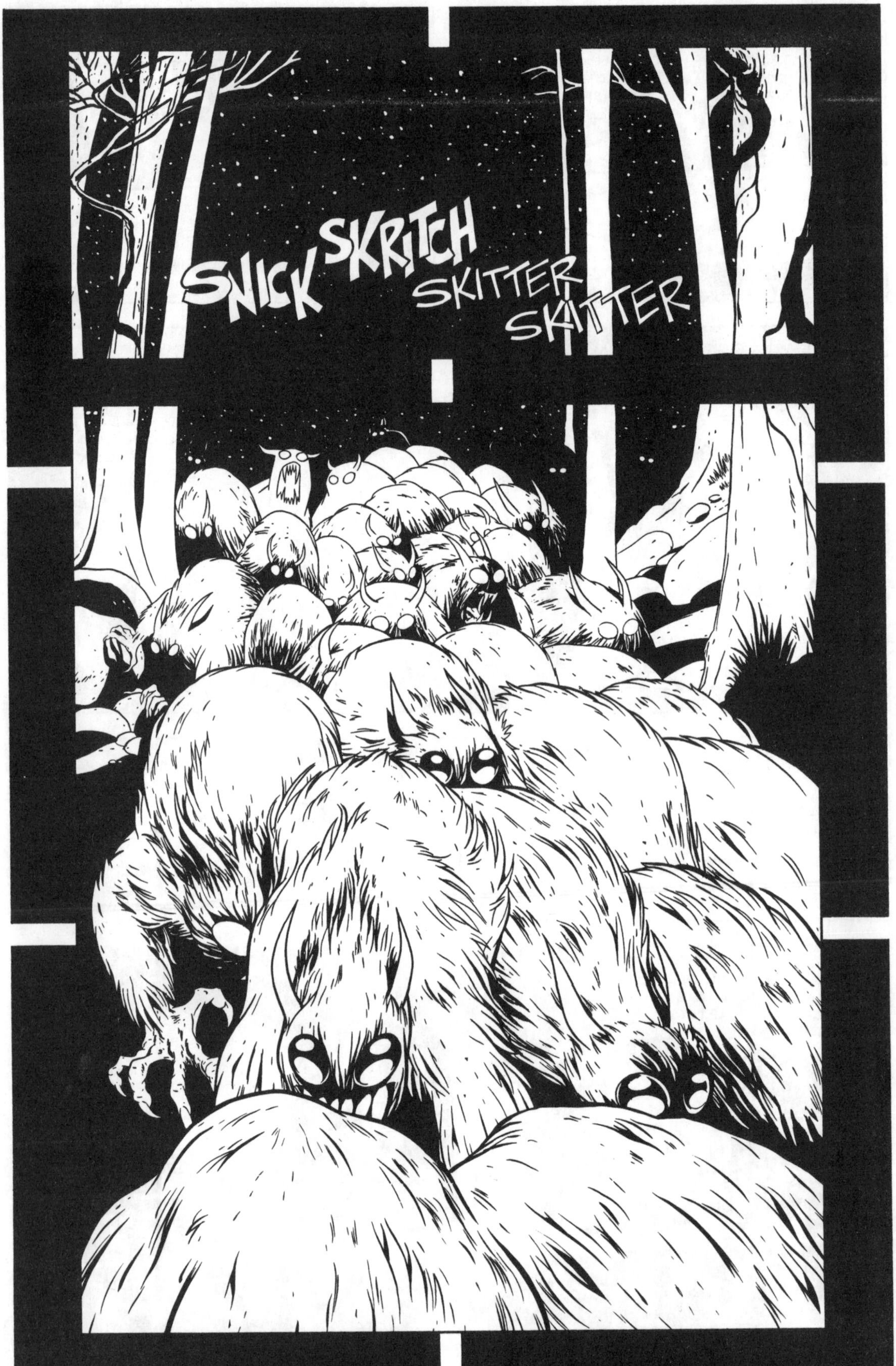
SNICK SKRITCH
SKITTER
SKITTER

97

UHHH

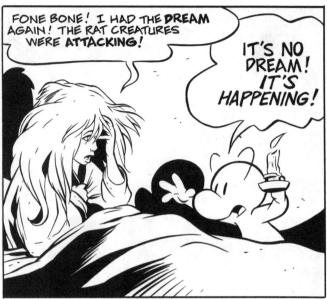

FONE BONE! I HAD THE **DREAM** AGAIN! THE RAT CREATURES WERE **ATTACKING**!

IT'S NO DREAM! IT'S HAPPENING!

NO--

THE RAT CREATURES HAVE SURROUNDED TH' FARM!! HURRY! GRAN'MA'S WAITING FOR US DOWNSTAIRS!

NEXt: TRAPPED

HOW MANY ARE THERE?

DON'T KNOW... HERE, BONE. HOLD THIS!

OH, MAN! I CAN HEAR 'EM MOVIN' **AROUND** OUT THERE!

THORN, DEAR... BRING ME A POKER FROM THE FIREPLACE -- AND YOU BETTER PUT SOME **SHOES** ON...

DO YOU HAVE A **PLAN**, GRAN'MA?

I HAVE AN IDEA THAT MIGHT WORK.

OKAY, CHILDREN! LISTEN CLOSELY! THIS IS WHAT WE'RE GOING TO DO...

-- WHEN I SAY RUN... ..., YOU **RUN**! GOT THAT?

WHAT?! THAT'S YOUR **PLAN**? RUN **WHERE**?

READY? HERE WE GO!

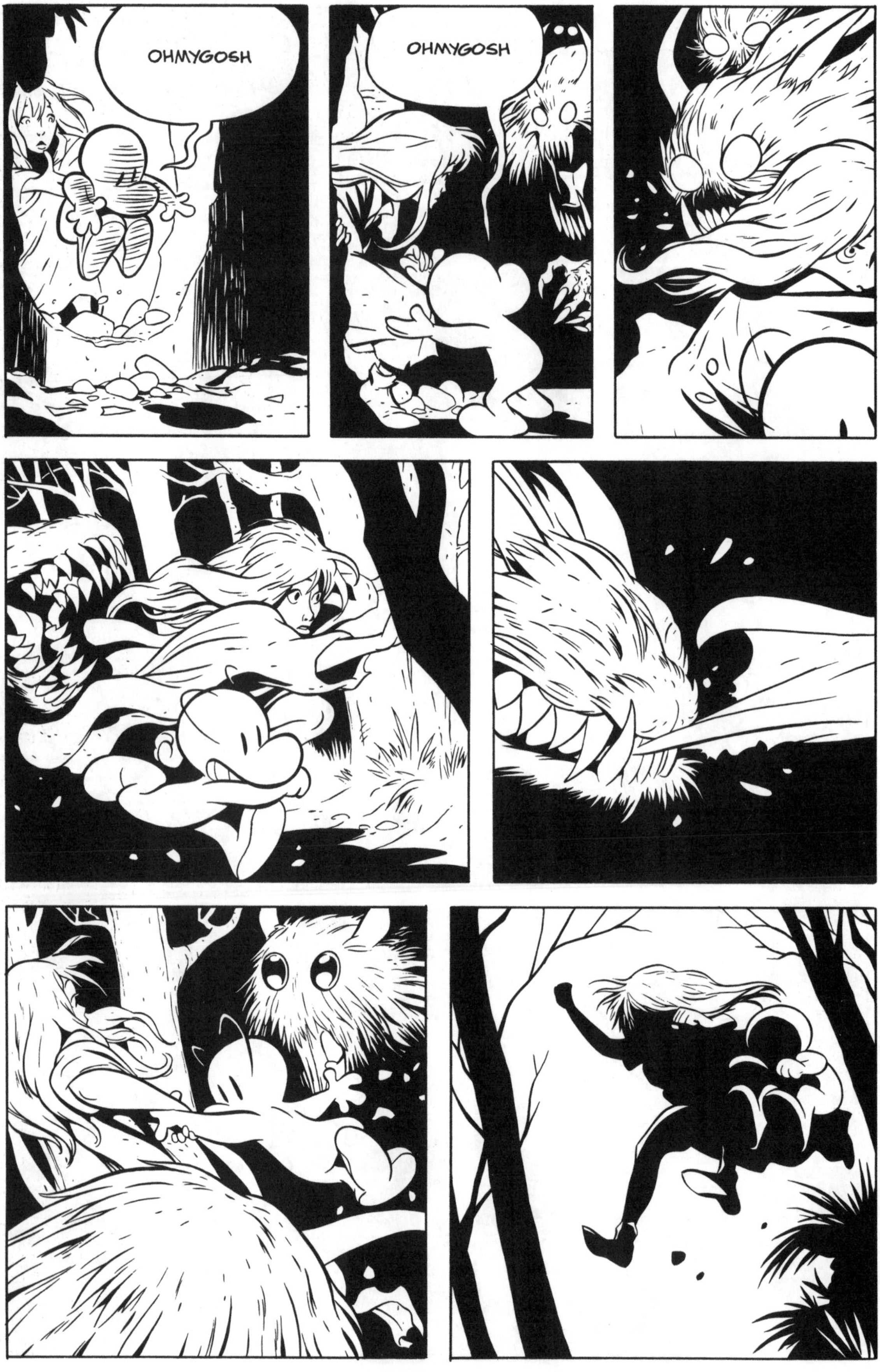
OHMYGOSH
OHMYGOSH

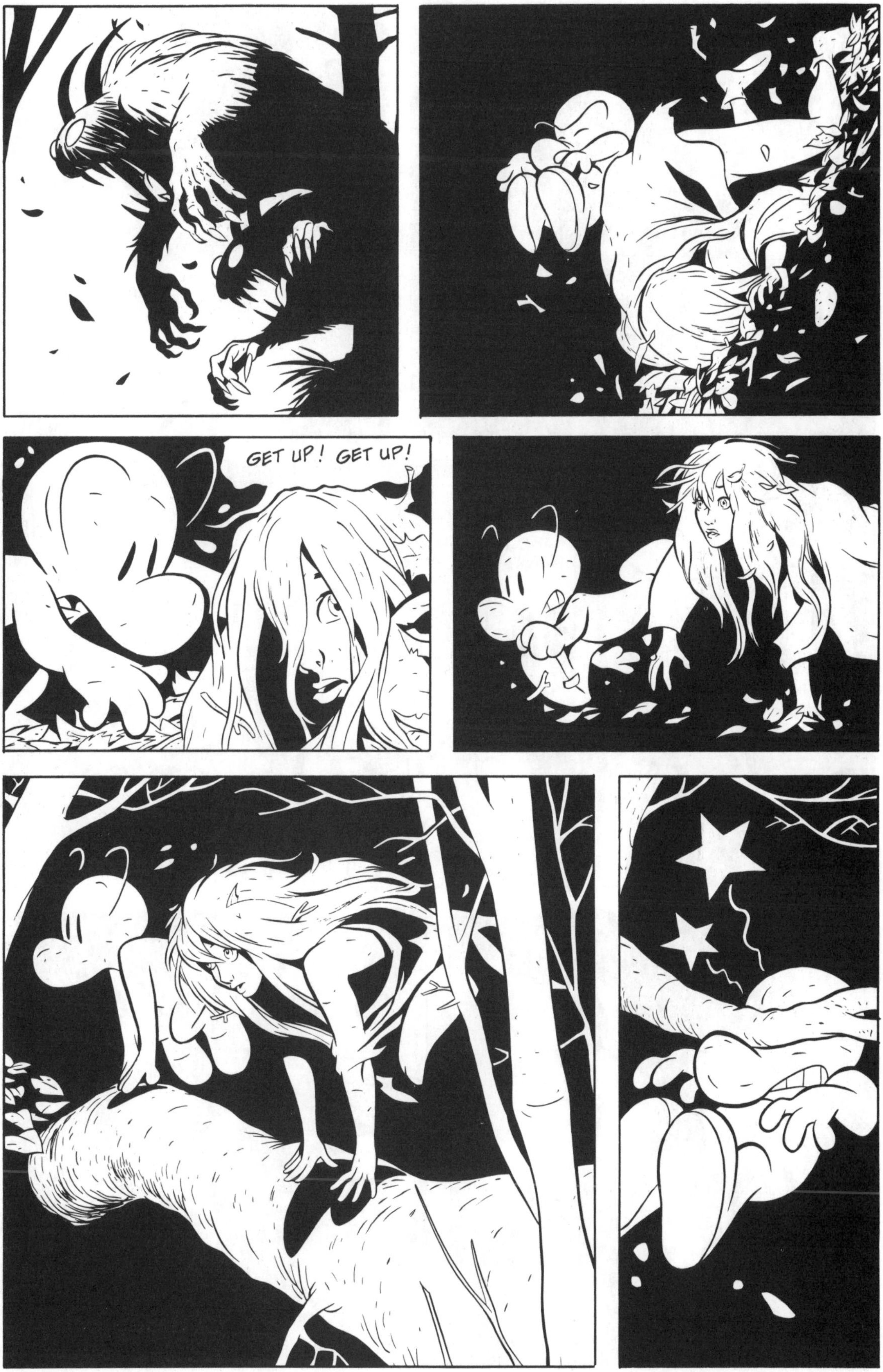
GET UP! GET UP!

104

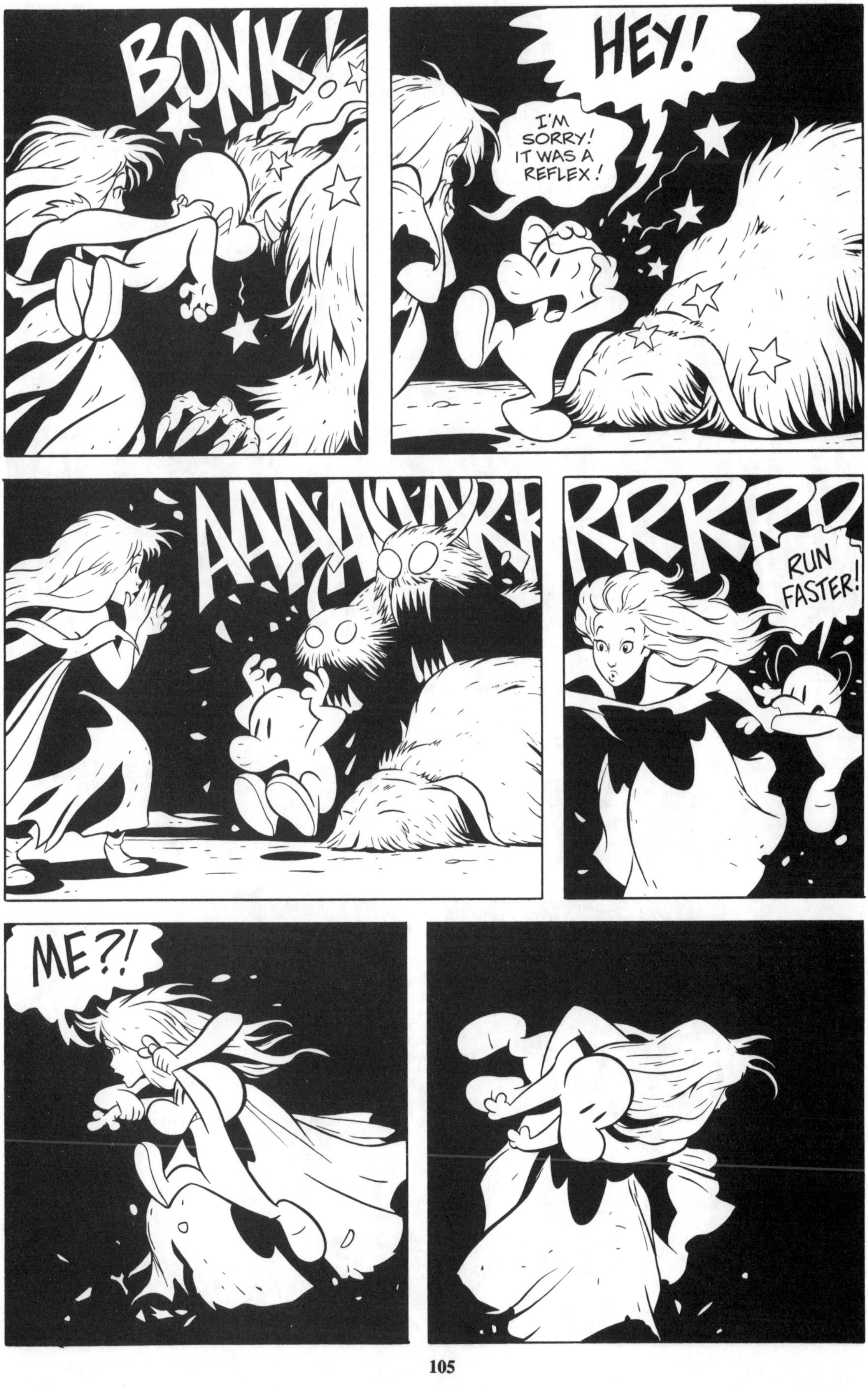
BONK!
HEY!
I'M SORRY! IT WAS A REFLEX!
AAAAAARRRRRRRR
RUN FASTER!
ME?!

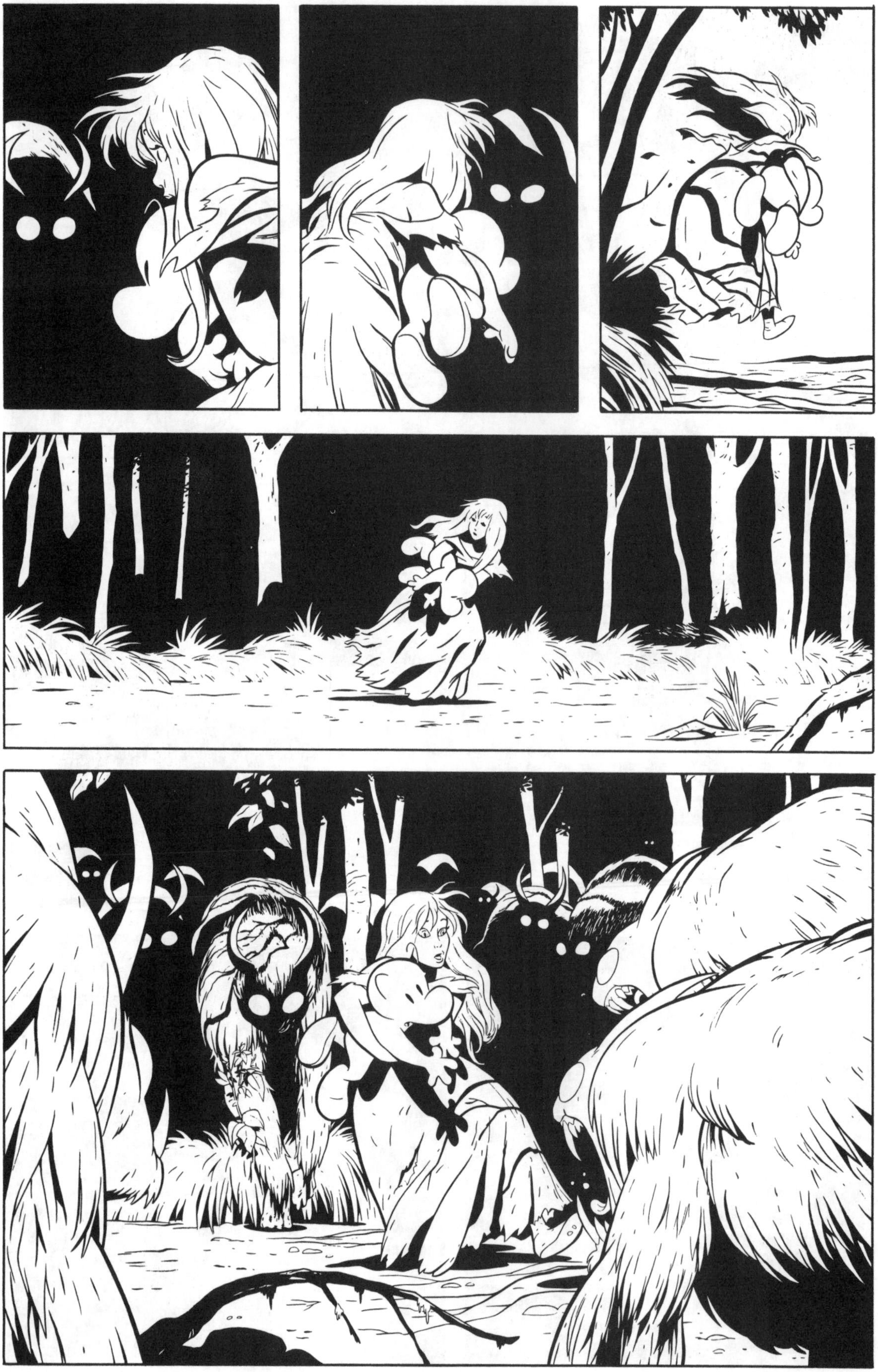

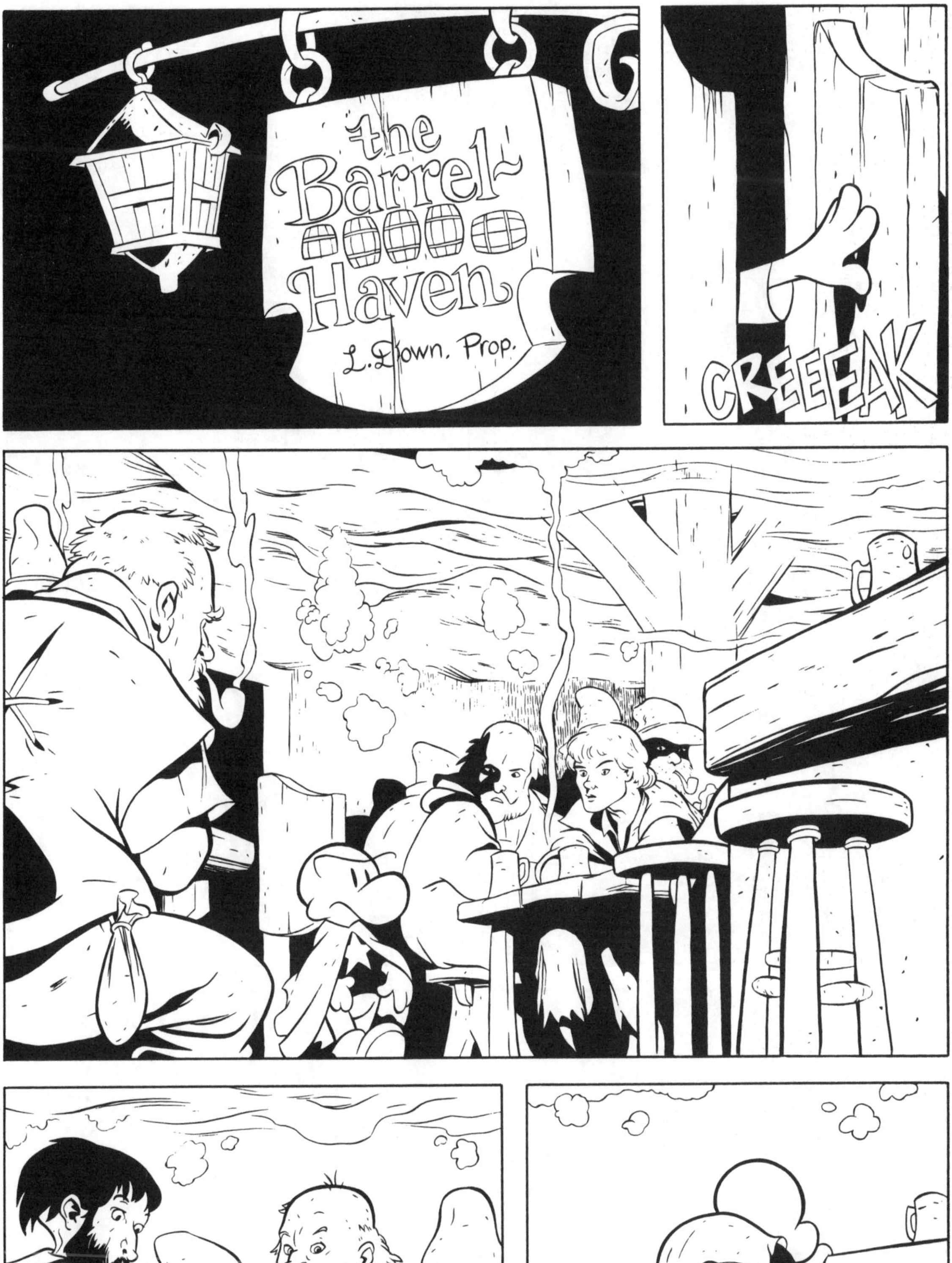
the Barrel Haven
L. Down. Prop.
CREEEAK

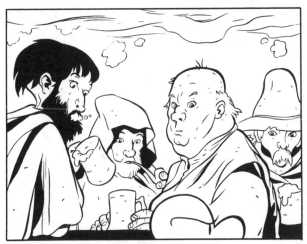

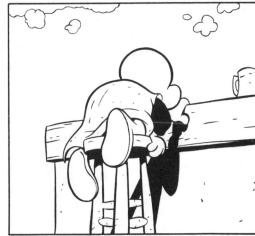

IT **IS** YOU! THANK **GOODNESS** I'VE **FOUND** YOU!!

YA **MEAN** IT, PHONEY? YOU'RE **HAPPY** TO SEE ME?

DARN RIGHT!! FONE BONE WOULDN'T LET ME **LEAVE** THIS STUPID VALLEY UNLESS I **FOUND** YOU FIRST!

AW, SHUCKS-- IT'S GOOD TO SEE YOU **TOO,** CUZ!

THIS CALLS FOR A **TOAST!** LET ME BUY YOU A **DRINK,** OL' **BUDDY!**

OKAY BY **ME,** OL' **PAL!**

HERE'S TO GOIN' **HOME!**

TO **BONEVILLE!**

CLINK

TO **BONEVILLE!**

GLUG! GLUG!

AHH!

WHADDYA SAY WE HAVE ANOTHER ROUND ON **YOU,** OL' **FRIEND!**

SMEK SMEK

SURE! WHY NOT? I GOT A FEELIN' MY **LUCK'S** ABOUT TO **CHANGE!** -- **GUESS** WHERE FONE BONE IS **RIGHT NOW!** HE'S WITH **GRAN'MA BEN!** YOU KNOW -- TH' OLD LADY THAT RACES **COWS!**

AH! YOU'RE IN TOWN FOR TH' **COW RACE!** ME TOO! THERE'S GONNA BE SOME HEAVY **BETTIN'** GOIN' ON!

SO I'VE HEARD!

IS ANYBODY DOIN' TH' **BOOKMAKIN'**?

NOT YET....BUT FROM WHAT I'VE PICKED UP--- YOUR FRIEND **GRAN'MA** IS TH' **ODDS ON** FAVORITE!

GREAT! PERFECT! HOW MUCH TIME DO WE HAVE?

ONE WEEK.

EXCELLENT! I GOT AN **IDEA** THAT'LL MAKE US A **LOTTA** MONEY!

UH, OH! I HOPE THIS ISN'T GONNA BE ONE OF THOSE **SILLY** IDEAS YOU USED TO PULL BACK IN **BONEVILLE**!

WHAT?! WHAT ARE YOU **TALKIN'** ABOUT? **WHAT** SILLY IDEAS?!

REMEMBER TH' **FIRST** TIME YOU GOT US RUN OUT OF TOWN? YOU OPENED UP A CHAIN OF FRANCHISES-- **BONE ENVIRONMENTAL:** NUCLEAR REACTOR AND ENDLESS SALAD BARS!

THAT WASN'T A **SILLY IDEA!** TH' **LETTUCE** WOULDN'T SPOIL FOR **DECADES!**

WHAT ABOUT TH' **SECOND** TIME YOU GOT US RUN OUT? WHEN YOU STARTED **THE NEW AGE SCHOOL OF LAMAZE AND BUNGY-JUMPING!** EVEN I KNEW **THAT** WAS DUMB!

OH, YEAH, YOU'RE A **BRILLIANT** JUDGE!

NOW-- WHERE ARE WE GONNA FIND YOU A **COW SUIT**?

WHAT? I GET TO WEAR A COW SUIT?! COOL! HAVE ANOTHER **BEER,** PARTNER!

KEEP IT **DOWN**, YOU CORN HEAD! I DON'T WANT ANYBODY TO KNOW WE'RE **TOGETHER**!

OH! RIGHT! **GOTCHA**!

OH, NO! NOT ANOTHER ONE.!! YOU BETTER BE ABLE TO **PAY** FOR THOSE BEERS, SHORTY!

DON'T WORRY! I'LL PRETEND I DON'T KNOW YOU... HUM TE DUM ♪

THAT'S **FIVE MUGS** OF MY **BEST ALE!** YOU OWE ME **TWO EGGS**, AN' I WANT IT **NOW!**

RELAX, KING KONG! I'M GOOD FOR IT!

DOO, DOO!

JUST LIKE THIS **OTHER** IDIOT WAS **GOOD** FOR IT?!

OH, MY! LOOK AT ALL THESE DIRTY GLASSES!

I'VE HAD IT UP TO **HERE** WITH YOU DRIFTERS COMIN' INTO TOWN FOR TH' FESTIVAL-- TRYIN' TO GET **BEER** ON **CREDIT!**

QUIT BREATHIN' IN MY **CUP!**

IT'S **MY** CUP UNTIL YOU PAY ME THE **TWO EGGS** YOU OWE ME!!

JEEZ! WHAT A **HOTHEAD!** HERE! TAKE IT!

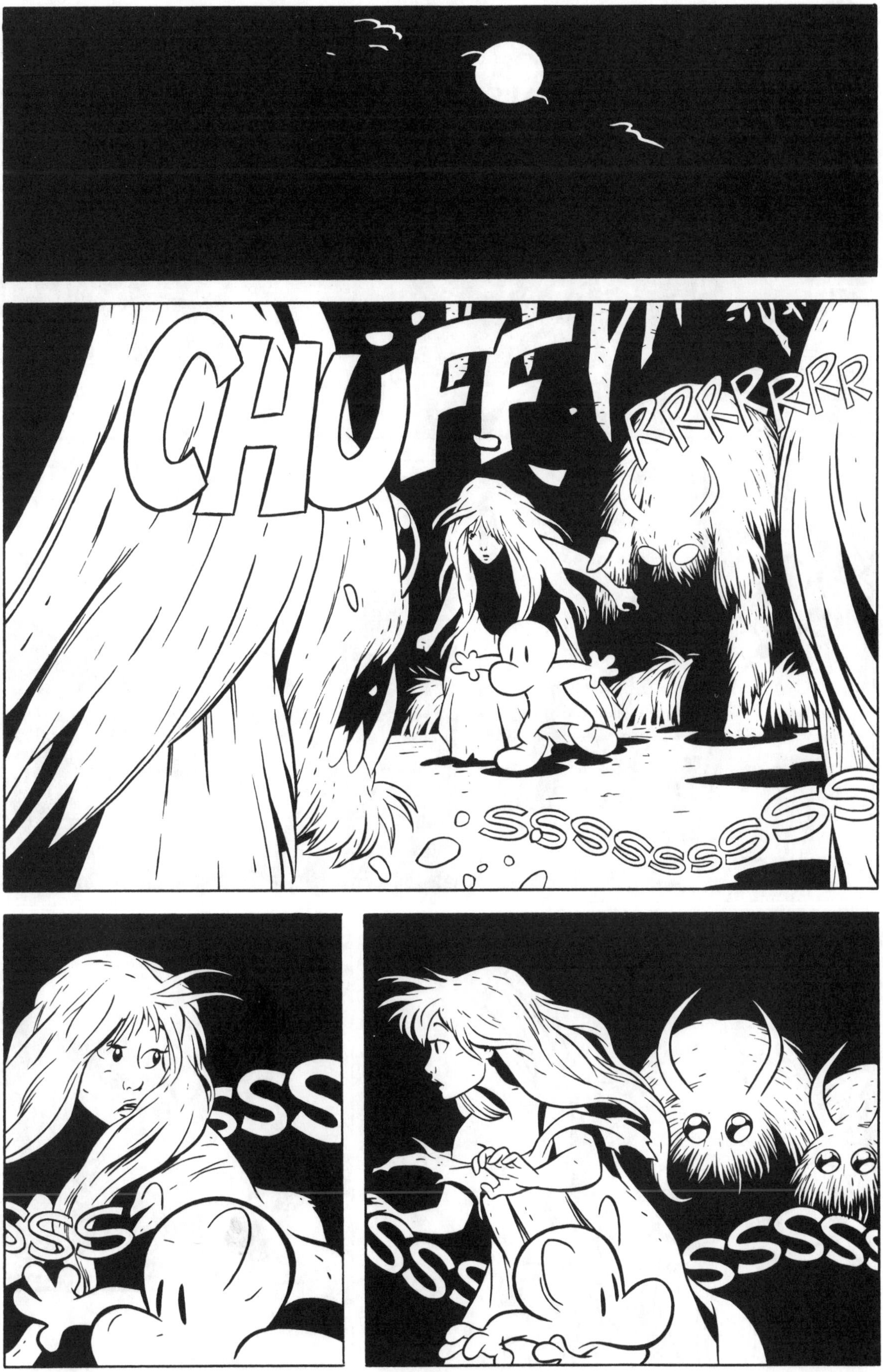
CHUFF
RRRRRRRR
SSSSSSSSSS
SSS
SSS
SSSSS
SSS

114

....DEFIANCE WILL NOT BE TOLORATED........ ....ONCE **WE** RETURN ORDER TO THE VALLEY......

STAY BACK!

SNIFF! SNIFF!

WAIT A MINUTE! WAIT A MINUTE!

DO YOU **SMELL** THAT?!

IT'S BRIMSTONE! IT'S THE **DRAGON!** HE'S **HERE!**

OH, NO.

RELAX, THORN! EVERYTHING'S GONNA BE **OKAY!**

FONE BONE! WHAT ARE YOU DOING?!

I KNOW **YOU** DON'T BELIEVE IN DRAGONS, BUT **THESE** GUYS DO! WATCH **THIS!**

OKAY, FELLAS! PARTY'S **OVER**! BREAK IT UP! **LET'S GO!** TH' DRAGON'LL BE HERE **ANY MINUTE** NOW, AN' YOU DON'T WANNA **BE** HERE WHEN HE SHOWS UP!

JUST THE **SIGHT** OF TH' DRAGON SENDS THESE GUYS INTO A **PANIC!** THEY RUN LIKE THEIR **FUR'S** ON FIRE!

ARE YOU STILL **HERE**? GO ON! **SHOO!**

I SMELL NOTHING...

WHAT ARE YOU **TALKIN'** ABOUT? YOU DON'T SMELL BRIMSTONE?

SSSSS

NO.

SNIFF! SNIFF! **THAT'S WEIRD!** I DON'T SMELL IT ANYMORE, EITHER!

LOOK OUT!

AARR

OOF!

CHUNK

117

HE **DID** IT! YES! I **TOLD** YOU THERE WAS A DRAGON! I **TOLD** YOU!

MR. DRAGON...

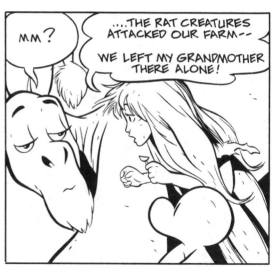

MM?

....THE RAT CREATURES ATTACKED OUR FARM--

WE LEFT MY GRANDMOTHER THERE ALONE!

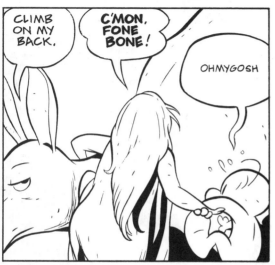

CLIMB ON MY BACK.

C'MON, FONE BONE!

OHMYGOSH

HOLD TIGHT!

HURRY!

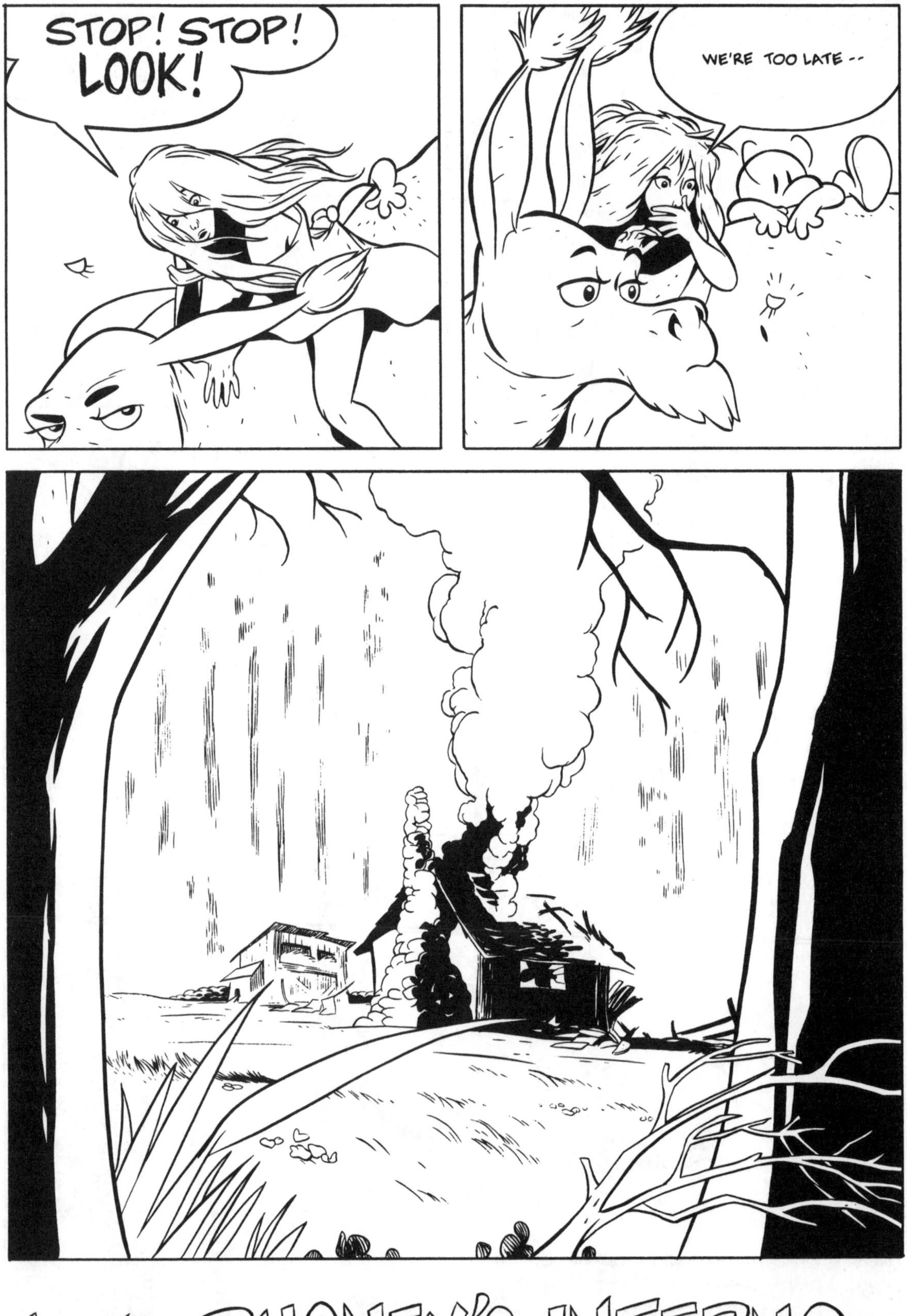
STOP! STOP! LOOK!
WE'RE TOO LATE --

Next: PHONEY'S INFERNO

122

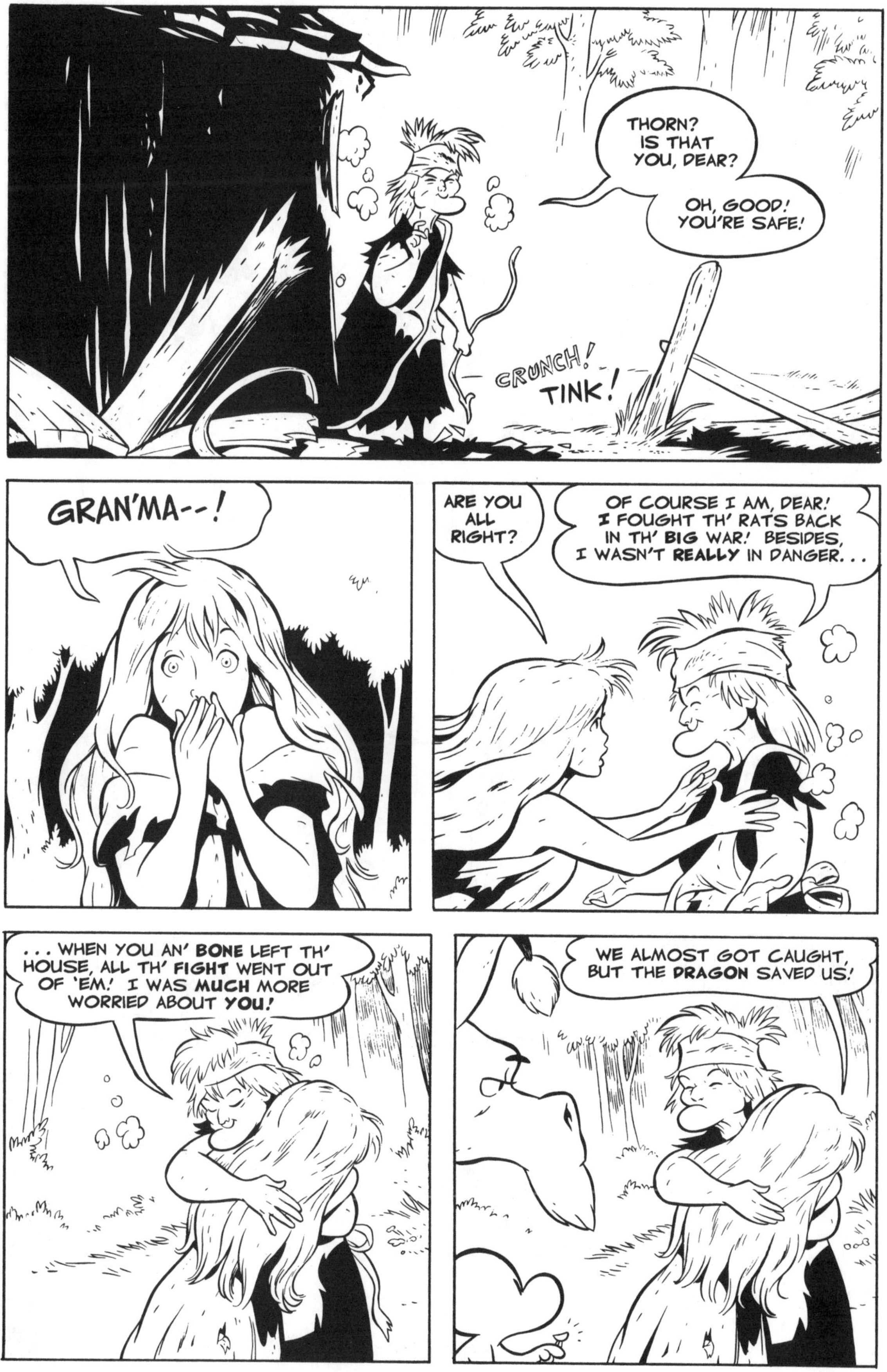
THORN? IS THAT YOU, DEAR?
OH, GOOD! YOU'RE SAFE!
CRUNCH!
TINK!
GRAN'MA--!
ARE YOU ALL RIGHT?
OF COURSE I AM, DEAR! I FOUGHT TH' RATS BACK IN TH' BIG WAR! BESIDES, I WASN'T REALLY IN DANGER...
...WHEN YOU AN' BONE LEFT TH' HOUSE, ALL TH' FIGHT WENT OUT OF 'EM! I WAS MUCH MORE WORRIED ABOUT YOU!
WE ALMOST GOT CAUGHT, BUT THE DRAGON SAVED US!

C'MON, TED.

GRAN'MA! WHAT ARE YOU **DOING**?! THE DRAGON JUST SAVED OUR **LIVES**!

NOT NOW, THORN. MR. BONE FROM BONEVILLE AN' I HAVE TO HAVE A LITTLE **CHAT**!

AND **YOU** HAVE A LOT OF THINGS TO DO BEFORE WE LEAVE FOR TH' **SPRING FAIR!**

THE **FAIR**?! YOU'RE NOT STILL WORRIED ABOUT YOUR **COW RACE**?!

WHAT ABOUT **PHONEY BONE** AN' **SMILEY**? WE HAVE TO **FIND** THEM!

BONE AND I WILL HITCH UP TH' CART. **YOU** BE A SWEETHEART AND PUT OUT TH' **FIRE** ON TH' ROOF!

SHE'S NOT EVEN **LISTENING** TO US! CAN YOU **BELIEVE** SHE WANTS TO GO TO TH' **FAIR**?!

ARE YOU **KIDDING**? I STILL CAN'T GET OVER TH' **FACT** THAT SHE HAS A **FIRST NAME!**

DEAR . . . I'M NOT A **COMPLETE** NINCOMPOOP! WE'LL BE **SAFER** IN **TOWN!** **AND**, WITH ANY LUCK, WE'LL BE ABLE TO FIND HIS **COUSINS!**

BUT — —

PLEASE, **THORN!** WE **HAVE** TO **GO!** WE DON'T KNOW IF THEY'RE **SAFE!**

YOU'RE RIGHT! I'LL TAKE CARE OF THE ROOF!

WE PACKED EVERYTHING LAST NIGHT, SO TH' LUGGAGE IS ALREADY OUT IN TH' BARN. COME JOIN US WHEN YOU GET DONE.

C'MON, BONE!

GRAN'MA? WHAT **WAS** THAT WITH YOU AN' TH' **DRAGON**? DO YOU GUYS **KNOW** EACH OTHER?

I'LL ASK TH' QUESTIONS! I WANNA KNOW WHY THOSE MONSTERS WERE AFTER **YOU** . . . AN' I WANT TH' **TRUTH!**

I HAVE **NO** IDEA! **HONEST!** I'VE NEVER DONE **ANYTHING** TO THEM!

WHAT ABOUT THAT SHIFTY **COUSIN** OF YOURS? YOU THINK **PHONEY BONE** MIGHT'VE HAD SOME DEALIN'S WITH 'EM?

NO, MA'AM! WE DON'T **HAVE** RAT CREATURES BACK WHERE WE COME FROM!

IN FACT, WE NEVER EVEN **HEARD** OF RAT CREATURES BEFORE WE GOT RUN OUT OF BONEVILLE!

WELL, ACTUALLY, I WASN'T RUN OUTTA BONEVILLE -- **PHONEY** WAS! SMILEY AN' I JUST HELPED HIM GET AWAY!

WHAT'D HE **DO?**

PHONEY DECIDED HE WAS GONNA RUN FOR **MAYOR!** HIS **CAMPAIGN** SLOGAN WAS: "AN' I'VE GOT TH' MONEY TO **DO** IT, TOO!"

SO TH' BONES RAN HIM OUTTA TOWN FOR **THAT,** HUH? WELL, **GOOD** FOR THEM!

NO. ANYBODY CAN RUN FOR MAYOR. EVEN **PHONEY!**

THAT GREEDY, LITTLE, **LOUDMOUTH?** NOT IN **MY** TOWN HE COULDN'T!

WELL, HE CAN IN BONEVILLE. **ANYWAY,** HE WANTED TO MAKE THE **OFFICIAL** ANNOUNCEMENT A BIG **SOCIAL EVENT,** SO HE DECIDED TO THROW A PICNIC DOWN ON TH' BANKS OF TH' **ROLLING BONE** RIVER . . .

THERE'S A **BEAUTIFUL** PARK THERE WITH GREEN, SLOPING LAWNS THAT STRETCH TO THE EDGE OF TH' WATER. IT'S JUST FAR ENOUGH AWAY FROM TH' **HUSTLE** AN' **BUSTLE** OF DOWNTOWN BONEVILLE THAT THERE WOULDN'T BE ANY **DISTRACTIONS!**

PHONEY INVITED **EVERYBODY** IN TOWN - - AN' HE PROMISED **FREE FOOD** FOR ANYONE WHO SHOWED UP! PRETTY SOON, TH' PICNIC WAS TH' **TALK** OF **BONEVILLE!**

THEN TH' **BIG** DAY ARRIVED, AN' TH' **WHOLE TOWN** TURNED OUT! TH' KIDS WERE PLAYIN' UNDER TH' TREES, AN' THE WOMEN WORE SUN-BONNETS AN' FANCY DRESSES! THE PICNIC WAS OFF TO A **PERFECT START!**

THERE'S A **STATUE** IN TH' PARK OF BONEVILLE'S **FOUNDER - - "BIG" JOHNSON BONE - -** AN' SINCE MY COUSINS AN' I ARE **DESCENDANTS** OF HIS, PHONEY WANTED TO MAKE HIS ANNOUNCEMENT IN FRONT OF TH' STATUE.

. . . AND JUST TO **ADD** TO TH' FESTIVITIES, PHONEY HAD A **50**ft. **BALLOON** MADE OF HIMSELF! TH' BALLOON WAS TIED TO OL' **"BIG" JOHNSON!**

FASTEN THAT END THERE, WOULD YOU, BONE?

EVERYTHING WAS GOIN' **GREAT!** FOLKS WERE LISTENIN' TO TH' **FIRE-HOUSE** BAND AN' ENJOYIN' TH' SUNSHINE! TH' FOOD WAS PASSED OUT AN' THERE WERE PLENTY OF **PRUNE TARTS** FOR **EVERYONE!**

PRUNE TARTS?

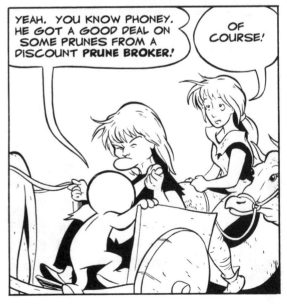

YEAH. YOU KNOW PHONEY. HE GOT A GOOD DEAL ON SOME PRUNES FROM A DISCOUNT **PRUNE BROKER!**

OF COURSE!

SO ANYWAY, HE MAKES THE **ANNOUNCEMENT**, RIGHT? HE GETS UP AND DECLARES HIS CANDIDACY FOR **MAYOR** OF **BONEVILLE**!

I STILL THINK **THAT'S** WHEN THEY SHOULD'VE RUN HIM OUT!

THAT'S WHEN A GUST OF WIND CAME OFF TH' **RIVER** AND PULLED TH' **BALLOON** LOOSE! THE STATUE CAME OFF ITS **BASE** AN' WAS DANGLIN' OFF TH' **BALLOON'S ANKLE**! ALL OF A **SUDDEN**, THIS GIANT, INFLATABLE PHONEY BONE STARTED MOVING TOWARD THE **CROWD**!

OH, MY!

YEAH, IT WAS **AMAZING**! MY FIRST-GRADE TEACHER, **MISS CRAB-BONE**, WAS THE FIRST TO **PANIC**! SHE STARTED SCREAMING AND RUNNING BACK AN' FORTH! THE BALLOON CHASED HER INTO TH' **RIVER** BEFORE SMILEY AND I COULD LET THE AIR OUT OF IT!

...IT WAS **AWFUL**! EVERYONE WAS **STUNNED**! AT FIRST NOBODY MOVED! THEY JUST **SAT** THERE WITH THIS LOOK OF **HORROR** ON THEIR FACES!

AN' **THAT'S** WHEN THEY RAN YOU OUTTA TOWN.

NO. THAT'S WHEN TH' **BAD PRUNES** KICKED IN...

HEY, SMILEY! TAKE THAT TUB OF GLASSES BACK TO YOUR BUDDY! WE'RE OUT OF MUGS AGAIN!

YES, SIR, MISTER DOWN!

HEY, THERE, PHONEY! LUCIUS SAYS YA GOTTA WASH THESE, PRONTO! WE GOT A LOT OF THIRSTY CUSTOMERS OUT FRONT!

OF COURSE, I MAKE SURE EVERYBODY GETS A NEW, CLEAN MUG WITH EACH DRINK!

YEAH. I NOTICED.

GLUNK

130

...I JUST WANT YOU TO KNOW... I'VE BEEN **WORKING** ON **THE PLAN!** I BEEN SPREADIN' **RUMORS** ALL DAY THAT **GRAN'MA BEN** IS **TOO OLD** TO WIN TH' RACE THIS YEAR!

IS ANYBODY **BUYIN'** IT?

I'M TH' **BARTENDER!** THEY **GOTTA** BELIEVE ME!

THIS IS **TOO EASY!** WE'LL COVER ALL TH' **BETS,** AND THEN WHEN **GRAN'MA WINS,** WE'LL BE **RICH!**

OF COURSE, WHEN GRAN'MA GETS INTO **TOWN,** EVERYBODY'S GONNA **SEE** SHE'S **PERFECTLY FIT!**

I'VE GOT THAT COVERED WITH PHASE **TWO:**

THE MYSTERY COW!

A **COW** THAT WE'LL **BUILD UP** IN EVERYBODY'S IMAGINATION THAT CAN'T BE BEAT!

WAIT! IS THAT TH' PART WHERE I GET TO WEAR TH' **COW SUIT?!** OH, **JOY!**

YEAH, **THAT'S** TH' PART! BUT YOU'RE GONNA **THROW** TH' RACE! REMEMBER! WE **WANT** GRAN'MA BEN TO WIN!

WELL, **NATURALLY,** I'M LOOKING FORWARD TO WEARIN' A **COW SUIT -** - BUT WHAT DO **YOU** GET OUT OF IT? AFTER **ALL,** THE LOCALS DON'T USE **MONEY!** THEY TRADE **GOODS 'N' SERVICES!**

IT **DOES** SOUR MY PLANS FOR AMASSING A **HUGE** FORTUNE AND RETURNING TO **BONEVILLE** IN **TRIUMPH** ... STILL, THE PLAY IS TH' **THING!**

IF ALL THESE YOKELS HAVE ARE **POULTRY PRODUCTS,** THEN I'LL **TAKE IT!!**

BESIDES, I HAVE A **HANKERIN'** TO TAKE TH' PROPRIETOR OF THIS FINE ESTABLISHMENT TO TH' **CLEANERS!** YOU **WITH** ME?

SURE! IT DOESN'T MAKE ANY DIFFERENCE TO ME! BUT THEN... NOT MUCH **DOES!**

GOOD. NOW GET BACK OUT THERE AND KEEP SPREADIN' **RUMORS!**

AN' QUIT BRINGIN' ME DIRTY DISHES TO WASH!

PHONCIBLE P. BONE.....AT **LAST** I HAVE FOUND YOU.....

WHO, ME? HOW DO YOU KNOW MY NAME?

...YOU SHOULD BE GRATEFUL INDEED THAT YOUR FRIENDS INTERFERED ON YOUR BEHALF LAST NIGHT.... I AM FORCED TO USE MUCH MORE SUBTLE METHODS OF CONTACTING YOU....

WHAT TH' **HECK** ARE YOU **TALKIN'** ABOUT?

....YOUR COUSIN FONE BONE HAS AWAKENED THE GREAT RED DRAGON.....
....FOR THIS...
...I WILL **KILL** HIM.....

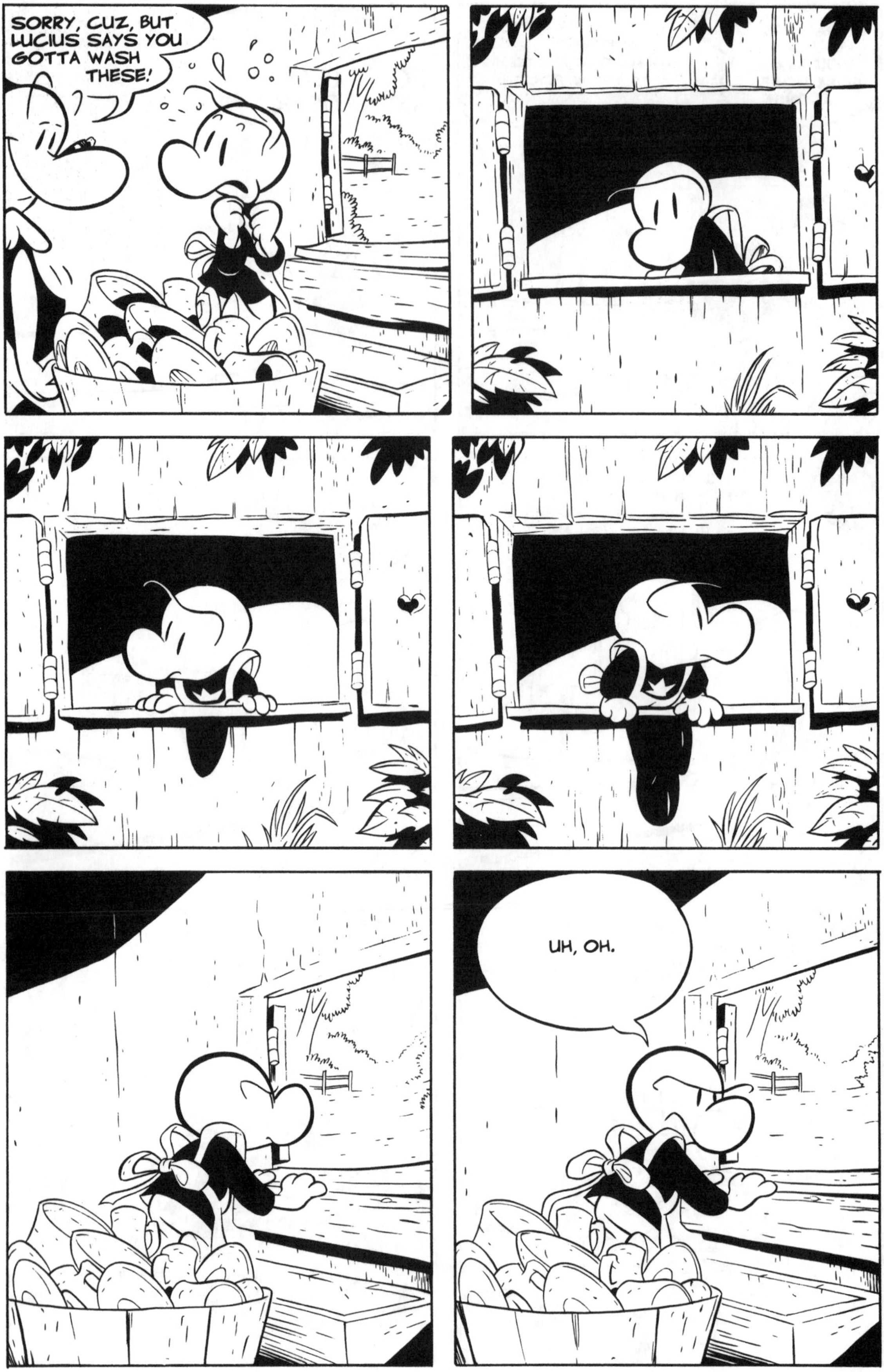
SORRY, CUZ, BUT LUCIUS SAYS YOU GOTTA WASH THESE!
UH, OH.

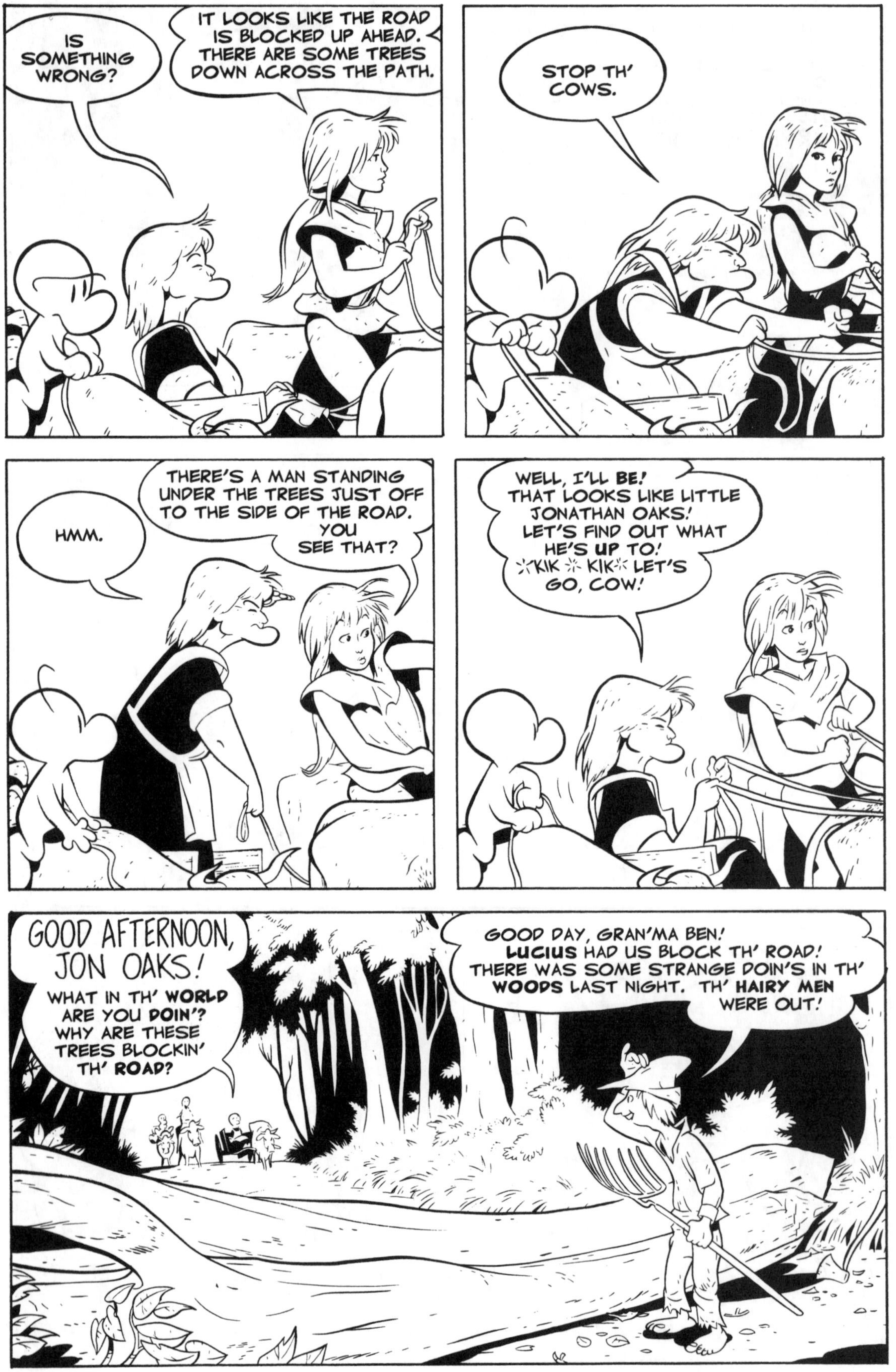

IS SOMETHING WRONG?
IT LOOKS LIKE THE ROAD IS BLOCKED UP AHEAD. THERE ARE SOME TREES DOWN ACROSS THE PATH.
STOP TH' COWS.
HMM.
THERE'S A MAN STANDING UNDER THE TREES JUST OFF TO THE SIDE OF THE ROAD. YOU SEE THAT?
WELL, I'LL BE! THAT LOOKS LIKE LITTLE JONATHAN OAKS! LET'S FIND OUT WHAT HE'S UP TO! KIK KIK LET'S GO, COW!
GOOD AFTERNOON, JON OAKS! WHAT IN TH' WORLD ARE YOU DOIN'? WHY ARE THESE TREES BLOCKIN' TH' ROAD?
GOOD DAY, GRAN'MA BEN! LUCIUS HAD US BLOCK TH' ROAD! THERE WAS SOME STRANGE DOIN'S IN TH' WOODS LAST NIGHT. TH' HAIRY MEN WERE OUT!

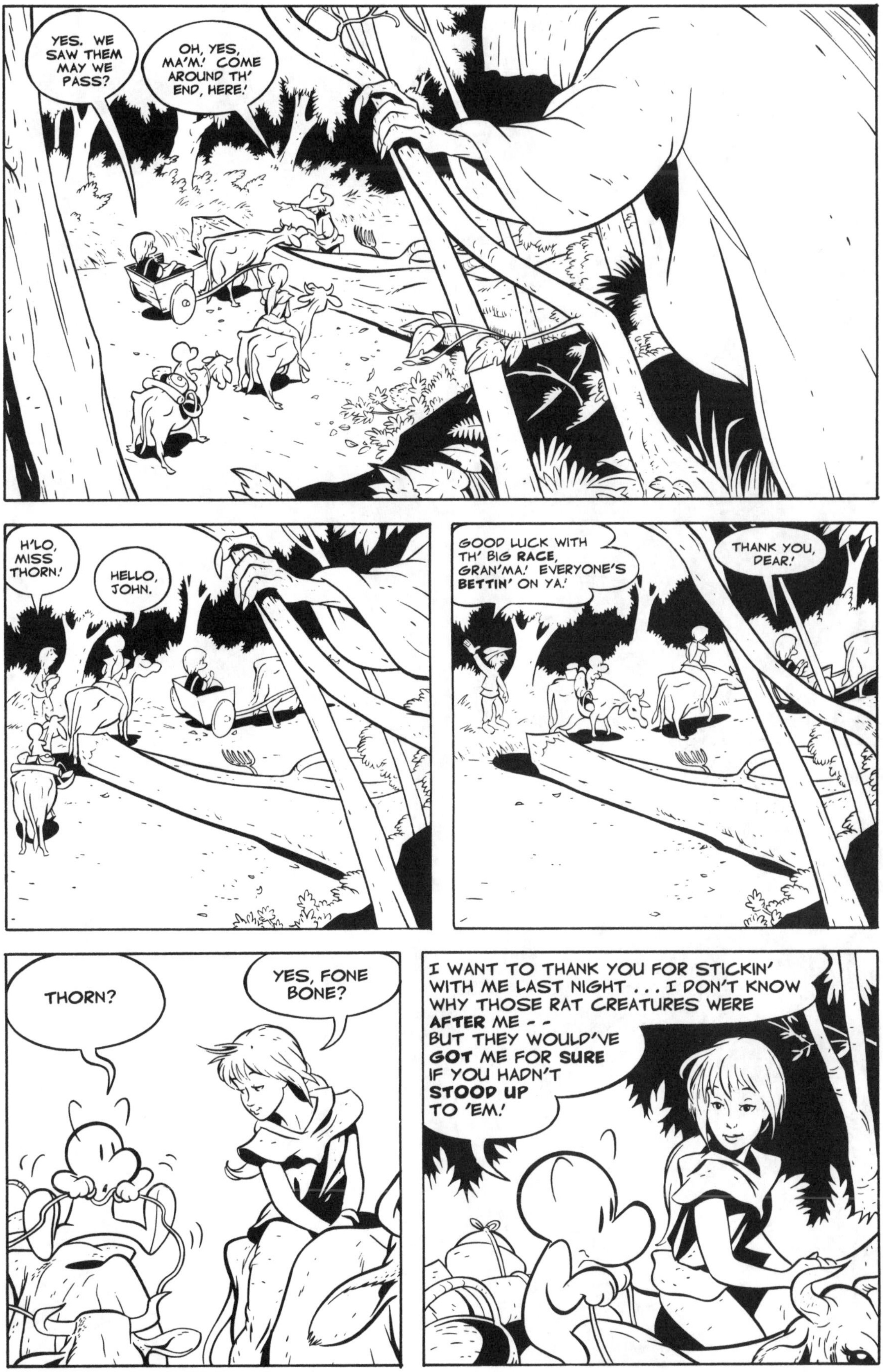
YES. WE SAW THEM MAY WE PASS?
OH, YES, MA'M! COME AROUND TH' END, HERE!
H'LO, MISS THORN!
HELLO, JOHN.
GOOD LUCK WITH TH' BIG RACE, GRAN'MA! EVERYONE'S BETTIN' ON YA!
THANK YOU, DEAR!
THORN?
YES, FONE BONE?
I WANT TO THANK YOU FOR STICKIN' WITH ME LAST NIGHT . . . I DON'T KNOW WHY THOSE RAT CREATURES WERE AFTER ME - - BUT THEY WOULD'VE GOT ME FOR SURE IF YOU HADN'T STOOD UP TO 'EM!

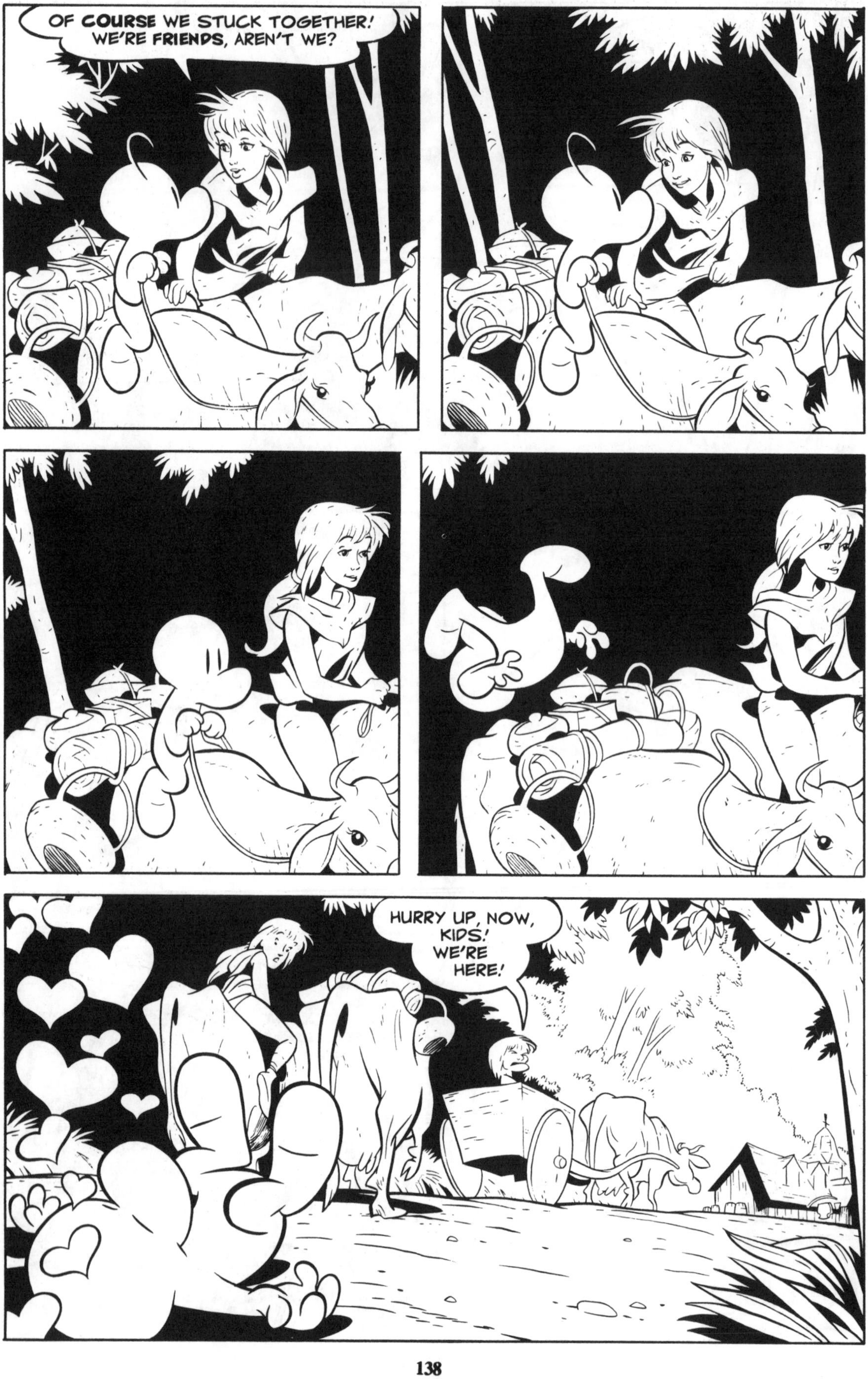
OF COURSE WE STUCK TOGETHER! WE'RE FRIENDS, AREN'T WE?
HURRY UP, NOW, KIDS! WE'RE HERE!

WELL, WELL . . . IT'S ABOUT **TIME**!

HELLO, LUCIUS!

HOW YA DOIN', ROSIE? WAS TH' **ROAD** SAFE? I WAS **WORRIED** ABOUT YA!

TH' ROAD WAS CLEAR . . . EXCEPT FOR YOUR **ROADBLOCK!**

OH! I GOT SOMETHIN' FOR YA! **HERE!** I BEEN SAVIN' IT IN MY POCKET ALL DAY!

OH, AREN'T YOU SWEET!

. . . WELLL . . . . . I HAD A LITTLE EXTRA **TIME** ON MY HANDS THIS MORNING . . .

. . . I GOT A COUPLE OF **DEAD BEATS** INSIDE TAKIN' CARE OF TH' **CUSTOMERS** -- IN FACT, THEY LOOK A **LOT** LIKE THIS LITTLE FELLA YOU GOT HERE.

THEY **DO?!**

141

NEXT: THE SPRING FAIR!